CABIN TRIPPING

CABIN TRIPPING

Where to Go to Get Away from It All

JJ Eggers

WRITTEN BY ALEXIS LIPSITZ

ARTISAN | NEW YORK

It's always been about more than just four walls and a roof. This is for everyone looking for a change of pace.

Library of Congress Cataloging-in-Publication Data

Names: Eggers, J. J., author.
Title: Cabin tripping : where to go to get away from it all / JJ Eggers.
Description: New York : Artisan, a division of Workman Publishing Co., Inc. [2021] | Includes index.
Identifiers: LCCN 2021015884 | ISBN 9781579659905 (Hardcover)
Subjects: LCSH: Vacation homes—Guidebooks. | Resorts—Guidebooks.
Classification: LCC TX907 .E33 2021 | DDC 643/.25—dc23
LC record available at https://lccn.loc.gov/2021015884

Design by Nina Simoneaux

Artisan books are available at special discounts when purchased in bulk for premiums and sales promotions as well as for fund-raising or educational use. Special editions or book excerpts also can be created to specification. For details, contact the Special Sales Director at the address below, or send an e-mail to specialmarkets@workman.com.

For speaking engagements, contact speakersbureau@workman.com.

Published by Artisan
A division of Workman Publishing Co., Inc.
225 Varick Street
New York, NY 10014-4381
artisanbooks.com

Artisan is a registered trademark of Workman Publishing Co., Inc.

Published simultaneously in Canada by Thomas Allen & Son, Limited

Printed in China

First printing, October 2021

10 9 8 7 6 5 4 3 2 1

CONTENTS

Waney Cabin has a leafy perch in the ancient forestlands of the Campwell Woods village (see page 40).

INTRODUCTION

"It is good to know that out there, in a forest in the world, there is a cabin where something is possible, something fairly close to the sheer happiness of being alive."

—Sylvain Tesson

The rental cabins featured in this book come in all shapes and sizes. Some are classic A-frames, restored to their mid-century glory or reimagined with modern updates. Some are steel-and-glass marvels—minimalist dreams that let their natural surroundings sing. Others are unexpected DIY dwellings, fashioned out of reclaimed wood, mud and straw, even used shipping containers. What they all share is a warm, wild spirit.

I chose these seventy-nine cabins not only for their authentic style and soulful interiors but also for their deep connection to incredible wild settings. The cozy cabin in the woods symbolizes the quintessential sanctuary of hearth, home, and bewitching enchantments. The curl of wood smoke rising from the chimney, the scent of pine, the promise of respite from a cold, flinty world: Cabins have a special place in our collective romantic heart.

The cabin culture of yore has been born again, fueled by the DIY revolution, the quest for authenticity and eco-conscious living, and a deep craving for a connection to nature. Individual homeowners and short-term-rental companies alike have grown to meet this need, offering intimate, singular experiences in idyllic wilderness settings. The little cabin that Grandpa built is now open to all—which means this book holds a lifetime of amazing travel itineraries. Let these cabins be your stepping-stones to seeing the world, whether that means watching the northern lights dazzle from a glass house in Iceland or observing whales cruising the Oregon coast.

I love cabins and everything they stand for. I love the chalets and ski huts of the European Alps, and the hand-built log cabins of the Midwest. I love the surf-shack mentality on the Philippines' tropical islands. I love the fact that a treehouse in Ontario has a slide that delivers you to the bottom, and that in Dolores, Colorado, you can stay in a genuine nineteenth-century cabin built by a gold-rush homesteader. I love that people would rather integrate their cabins into the natural landscape than cut down even one tree, ending up with big oaks growing out of decks and with leafy canopies of natural shade.

That my livelihood centers around cabins was never planned; it sort of snuck up on me. I've lived in and around the Wasatch Mountains of Utah my entire life. My siblings and I spent our childhood hiking, snowboarding, and skiing. I understood from an early age how good it feels to be out in the wild—and I encountered my share of beautiful cabins along the way. At some point, I started collecting photos of my favorites on my phone. I developed an appreciation for the architecture and history of cabins, and my love of wild places only deepened.

Eventually I built my Instagram page, @TheCabinChronicles, to share these spectacular places I had been saving (and obsessing over). The next thing I knew, I had a growing audience of engaged followers who, like me, were discovering a passion for cabins they never knew they had.

A cabin in the woods is more than shelter. It's a sanctuary from the stress of modern life. It's a call to nature. It's where we get back to ourselves and one another. It doesn't have to be an original Frank Lloyd Wright or showcase the latest in hot-tub technology: the standard-issue wood cabin with a fire roaring, a comfy chair, the glow of fairy lights, and the natural world just outside is fine by me. In fact, it doesn't get any better than that.

—JJ Eggers

Grey Duck Cabin,
page 83

Forest

TREEHOUSE A-FRAME

Now, *this* is a deck with a view. The Treehouse A-Frame is spacious and sprawling, built into the sun-dappled canopy on 4 acres (1.6 ha) of the Shasta-Trinity National Forest. Your views include Shasta Lake, where granite peaks rise above glittering blue waters.

This solid-built A-frame retreat on wooded land is designed for easy living. The main room is a warm honeycomb of knotty pine, with a wood-burning stove, vintage wicker chairs, and an antique desk; strings of fairy lights illuminate the wood-beamed ceiling. In the bathroom, a twee one-person tub is tucked into a windowed eave. Turn off your phone (cell service is limited anyway) and your computer (Wi-Fi is iffy, too) and turn up the tunes: When the fog rolls in and a fire is crackling, the cabin's collection of vinyl only adds to the magic.

Nearby, a 4-mile (6.4 km) round-trip hike along the McCloud River Trail passes three falls as it winds upstream among forested canyonland. The Hirz Bay boat launch, leading to Shasta Lake, is just 4 miles (6.4 km) from the cabin. The lake buzzes with boaters, anglers, and water-skiers.

For a more relaxed hang, head to Whiskeytown Lake, part of the Whiskeytown National Recreation Area, 10 miles (16 km) away. There are no personal watercraft allowed, and it's prized for its high-visibility waters and seasonal recreation, from moonlight kayaking to swimming.

You're also close to the recreation-rich peaks of the Cascade Range. Snow blankets the craggy onyx peaks of Mount Shasta, a forty-five-minute drive north, pretty much all year round—it's a cinematic beauty. Shasta is the second-highest mountain in the Cascades, at an elevation of 14,179 feet (4,322 m). It's also an active volcano that erupts an average of once every six hundred years. (Last eruption: more than two centuries ago.) The steep slopes draw climbers in summer and backcountry skiers in winter—skiing Avalanche Gulch from Mount Shasta's peak is a revered backcountry descent. The Mount Shasta Ski Park has boundless skiing and snowboarding terrain. And if you can't get enough of nature, three boffo national parks (Lassen Volcanic, Redwood, and Crater Lake) are each a few hours' drive away.

Ceiling beams strung with fairy lights and a wood-burning stove give the cabin a warm, cozy feel.

OPPOSITE The spacious A-frame has classic knotty-pine walls and a designated main bedroom in the loft space.

THE BOX HOP

Building a house out of shipping containers had been Seth Britt's dream since college. As housing costs rise and millions of used containers pile up in steel junkyards around the globe, it's recycling on an industrial scale, and cost effective to boot. So in 2019, Britt and his wife, Emily, bought 18.5 acres (7.5 ha) of dense pine-tree forest near rural Hocking Hills, Ohio, and went to work. Preparing a site in the middle of the woods was the first of many obstacles. "We had to clear the lot, dig a trench, install conduit for electrical, and dig a well," says Emily. And where does one go to buy a used shipping container? "Craigslist!"

Building with 40-foot-long (12 m) intermodal shipping containers poses its own interesting challenges. It took days of hard work just cutting windows and skylights into the steel exteriors. Wood siding was placed over framed areas, and the exposed steel was transformed with dark-green DTM (direct-to-metal) paint.

The results exceeded all expectations—the Box Hop has a great-looking contemporary style, helped by a slightly offset configuration and Emily's design chops. It's not huge, at 920 square feet (85 sq m), but the use of space is ingenious (the floor plan fits in three bedrooms). Inside are vintage rugs, a gas fireplace, and a gorgeous dining table that a friend built out of sycamore. A 16-foot (4.9 m) sliding glass door lets in copious tree-dappled light. The Box Hop also expands its footprint with loads of outdoor spaces, from a wraparound deck to a fire ring to a six-person hot tub. A rooftop patio accessed by a spiral staircase inside overlooks a forested ravine; the deck is made of interlocking pavers from recycled car tires.

In late 2019, the Britts snapped up two more used shipping containers to build the smaller BoHo Box Hop. The properties' beautiful acreage is ripe for wooded exploration and nature communing and is near both Hocking Hills State Park (and all its hiking, biking, fishing, and rock-climbing recreation) and the high cliffs and rugged gorges of Conkles Hollow State Nature Preserve.

e really drawn to
new life and recycling
g that would have
e been scrapped and
d again," says
r Emily Britt.

The spiral staircase leads to the second floor, where a third shipping container holds two bedrooms and a bathroom, and offers access to the rooftop patio.

The width of the house was doubled by opening up one container to another—and fusing them with a 22-foot (7 m) steel beam.

WOODHOUSE MUSKOKA

"One of the main reasons we bought a log house was because of its low environmental impact," says Jill Mandley, who along with her husband, Stephen Gardner, purchased Wood House Muskoka in 2018. Properly built, a log cabin home is one of the most sustainable forms of construction, using almost four times fewer fossil fuels in manufacturing than a conventional framed house. Wood is a natural insulator, and log cabins have a built-in energy efficiency that keeps a house warmer in winter and cooler in summer. A sealed log home is weather resistant, too, and solid log-wall construction is free of toxic chemicals or glues.

Aesthetically, the elegant simplicity of a log cabin is also hard to beat. The Wood House is warm and wonderful and everything you want a log cabin in the woods to be. The interior is two stories of golden-tinged, abundant space, with a custom split-log staircase leading to four bedrooms. The kitchen, a gut redo, is a model of smart Scandi style and modern efficiency, with hand-poured cement countertops, heated tile floors, and white cabinetry. A shimmering basket pendant light hangs above the lo-o-o-ng dining room table. Walls throughout are hung with rusticated grace notes, like antique oars and vintage crocheted blankets. The open-plan living area has a granite-faced wood-burning fireplace, but it's the massive white-pine logs that really impress. "Being in a log home is literally like living in a forest," Mandley says. "From the moment you walk inside the cabin, you feel this magical energy. It feels like home."

With 200 feet (61 m) of beautiful waterfront on the Severn River, the Wood House sits on 2 acres (0.8 ha) of mature pines, home to wild turkeys, white-tailed deer, red foxes, and owls. The secluded waterfront locale has a floating dock for swimming and fishing. Take a dip in the river, kayak or canoe, or watch the morning mist rise over the river from a hammock strung between trees.

GETAWAY FRAME

This is one honey of an A-frame. Generously sized, the cabin fits up to thirteen people, with three bedrooms and what may be an A-frame record: three full (and superstylish) bathrooms, two of them brand new. A fully outfitted baker's kitchen holds a Vitamix, an Instant Pot, and a Dutch oven, and the freezer comes stocked with a fresh batch of homemade chocolate chip cookie dough, ready to bake. That's right: *There's cookie dough in the freezer*.

The 2018 renovation of this 1970s cabin resulted in key structural improvements. The removal of a dropped ceiling overhanging the kitchen opened up a lofty vaulted expanse. Out went a large, unwieldy stone fireplace platform; in went a sleek wood-burning stove. New white metal and cedar-shake roofing mixed the chic and the folksy. Small windows got bigger. But it just may be the high-quality finishes that really light up the place—everywhere you look, there are tactile surfaces of marble, metal, leather, and weathered woods.

Among the A-frame's many crush-worthy elements: a kitchen island crafted from a vintage bowling lane, a big soaker tub under a bathroom skylight, and a staircase that seems to float. The great room is bathed in buttery sunshine from floor-to-ceiling windows, and high ceilings throughout allow for not one but two sets of triple twin bunk beds. The wraparound patio is big enough for a long dining table; the forested backyard holds a hammock or two. Custom touches abound, right down to the fresh-scented soaps and shampoos from Public Goods.

The posh comfort of the cabin matches its setting, a swath of woods in the Pinetop Country Club community. You're right in the heart of Arizona's White Mountains, with easy access to stellar hiking, mountain biking, kayaking, and fishing. The A-frame is a forty-five-minute drive from the Sunrise Park Resort, which boasts sixty-five downhill ski runs and a snowboarding terrain park (yes, you can ski—and ski well!—in Arizona); the resort is operated by the White Mountain Apache Tribe. But with space to spare, the hushed embrace of piney woods, and warm cookies, you may be happy just staying put.

The master-suite bathroom features a big white soaking tub beneath a skylight.

OPPOSITE This head-to-tail renovation includes an expanded deck and a stylish new roof combining cedar shake and white metal.

A BLACK
A-FRAME

Few places encapsulate the spirit of the A-frame revival more completely than this black beauty on 2 acres (0.8 ha) of Catskills forest. In 2015, the cabin got a full gut renovation and reconfiguration, which turned a dilapidated hunting lodge from the 1960s into a superstylish sanctuary. The dining table sits beneath original wood beams in the A-frame's cathedral pitch. A chef's kitchen is small but loaded with culinary toys. The cabin's two bedrooms are roomy and sunlit; the two private baths have soaking tubs and nifty black-and-white trompe l'oeil flooring.

Set back on a private road, the cabin has a large front deck that faces the woods. You can sit in the screened-in gazebo and listen to the forest music and watch the gentle rippling of the small spring-fed pond. Outside is a firepit and a picnic table under twinkling fairy lights strung from the trees.

The town of Kerhonkson, New York, is a modest hamlet of artists, farmers, and urban expats. Pick your own apples at Kelder's Farm and say hello to the third-largest gnome in the world, Gnome Chomsky. Or stop by the nearby Ashokan Reservoir, the mighty Catskills basin that delivers fresh water to the Big Apple, a two-hour drive away. The sprawl of blue water, with its backdrop of curvy black hills, is quite a sight.

If you're feeling adventurous, head to the Mohonk Preserve, 10 miles (16 km) from the A-frame in the Shawangunk Mountains, aka the Gunks, part of the Appalachian Mountains ridge. It's a playground for outdoor enthusiasts, with hiking and biking trails on 70 miles (113 km) of historic carriage roads and skiing on both groomed and backcountry trails. Eight thousand acres (3,237 ha) of quartzite cliffs make this a formidable rock-climbing destination, drawing climbers from around the world. Many of today's most-climbed routes were laid down by a rowdy group of college students known as the Vulgarians, who in the 1960s made daredevil ascents into the Gunks, often in sneakers and frequently in the nude, to protest efforts by the more buttoned-down Appalachian Mountain Club to control climbing access. The Vulgarians became legend, and climbing the Gunks in the buff turned into something of a rite of passage.

BOLT FARM
TREEHOUSE

If your idea of glamping leans toward the Southern Gothic, then these South Carolina treehouses are for you. The rooms are gussied up with chandeliers and sheepskin rugs and antiques. Tiers of transom windows give guests sun-dappled views of a Lowcountry tidal creek, all sultry Spanish moss and live oaks. You can lie in ornate hand-painted beds or bathe in big copper tubs while gauzy floor-length curtains billow in the soft breezes.

The owners of Bolt Farm, who bought 34 acres (14 ha) of Wadmalaw Island to develop a nature retreat, have created their treehouse kingdom for grown-ups with a heightened sense of play. The Wildflower Treehouse (pictured opposite) has fantastic chevron walls and a honey-hued color scheme, while the Honeymoon Treehouse is a fantasy in white, all poufs and fuzzy rugs and crystal chandeliers. The Charleston Treehouse features a wall of transom windows and has two outdoor soaking tubs for bathing à deux. The Living Room Treehouse is a cook's dream, equipped with a barbecue grill and a pizza oven. Outside is a private shower with two showerheads, a firepit, and a big deck for watching deer, foxes, and wild turkeys.

Wadmalaw Island calls itself the "back porch" of Charleston, just 30 miles (48 km) away—and a day trip into this beautiful city of well-preserved eighteenth- and nineteenth-century architecture is highly recommended. But you may be too bewitched by Wadmalaw's unspoiled charms to bother. The sleepy island has no grocery and no gas station and has restrictive land-use regulations meant to keep it that way. Still, civilization is within easy reach. You're a fifteen-minute drive to a supermarket, and the Ambrose Family Farm sells fresh produce in season from a stand on neighboring Johns Island; they also have a little café serving Lowcountry favorites like shrimp and grits. Wadmalaw has the last remaining tea farm in the United States, and a nearby distillery makes tea-flavored vodka. It's firewater with a homegrown feel, and that suits Wadmalaw just fine.

The Wildflower Treehouse has distinctive chevron walls, an outdoor bed swing, and tidal-creek views.

RIGHT *The Honeymoon Treehouse interior: It's as if someone dropped Scarlett O'Hara's boudoir into a fancy Victorian barn.*

BELOW AND OPPOSITE *Live oaks stretch over the exterior and deck of the Honeymoon Treehouse.*

JUST OUT OF NASHVILLE

Smithville,
Tennessee

This Smithville A-frame was originally a model cabin, built in the 1960s to help sell lots in the new lake community. Its unusual boatlike shape is a twist on the typical A-frame, with a rounded bow frame built of long pieces of curved timber, a style that dates back to medieval days. It may have started as a whimsical nod to the lake and its water-sports pleasures, but these days it's a chic and cozy escape in the woods.

When owners Kristin Barlowe and her husband, James, bought the property and its surrounding acre (0.4 ha) of forest, they could see the good bones behind the cabin's dated 1970s decor. Today sunlight pours in through big glass windows and doors in the lofted living area. The room is anchored by a stone wood-burning fireplace and a sculptural chandelier hanging from the cathedral ceiling. The big deck, complete with firepit, sectional, and picnic table, is a fabulous hub for hanging out under the leafy canopy. Modern comforts—Wi-Fi, central heating, AC, luxury linens—are legion, but the A-frame's retro-rustic soul shines throughout.

Even the exterior has a classic feel, painted a cool dark hue that changes from black to blue to forest green on the whims of the light.

Just a ninety-minute drive from Nashville, the cabin is nestled on a peninsula at Center Hill Lake, where the shoreline of craggy rock bluffs and waterfalls is mercifully undeveloped. Rent a fishing boat at the lake's Hidden Harbor Marina and go trawling for bass, catfish, bluegill, and walleye. You also have access to the community's hiking trails, a saltwater swimming pool, tennis courts—even a zip line through the woods.

Just down the street is Evins Mill and its dreamy swimming hole beneath a 90-foot (27 m) waterfall. Cumberland Caverns, with 30 miles (48 km) of underground caves, waterfalls, and pools, is forty-five minutes away by car. The forest trails of Rock Island and Burgess Falls State Parks are a ten-minute drive from the cabin. Smithville's own midsummer Fiddlers' Jamboree brings world-famous pickers and fiddlers to town and ends with a champion fiddle-off.

CAMPWELL WOODS

In a 40-acre (16 ha) pocket of storybook Cotswolds forest, this collection of log A-frames, handcrafted yurts, shepherd's hut, and cob roundhouse sends its guests back to simpler times. You can forage for edible plants, dine alfresco on fire-cooked meals, and sip "wild" cocktails. You can also partake in classic summer-camp activities: archery, canoeing, hiking—woodworking classes are even on offer. A lake in the woods makes a dreamy swimming hole, and long-limbed trees beckon for freewheeling climbs.

Campwell's festive collective feel attracts groups of friends and families, who favor the private suite of three adjoining yurts called the Chief's Den. The rest of the camp "village" shares a four-person wood-fired sauna, a bathhouse known as the Treeshack (with hot showers and composting toilets), and a communal outdoor kitchen with a wood-fired cob oven and grills. Of the village lodgings, the little one-room Waney Cabin, one of two rustic A-frames, looks out onto a forest path. Wooden steps with a charmingly crooked rail lead up to the other, a miniature log

A-frame named the Hairy Cabin for its crown of dense vegetation. The Cob Round is, as the name implies, a roundhouse, fashioned of cob, a mix of clay, sand, and straw that's been used to build dwellings since ancient times. It's breathable, thermal, and really durable (the oldest cob house on the planet is said to be ten thousand years old).

The closest village is the parish of Ashwicke, in the Cotswold wool country. Just 12 miles (19 km) away is Marshfield, a historic market town filled with seventeenth- and eighteenth-century architecture. From the camp, you have views of St. Catherine's Valley, a magical landscape of velvety hills and valleys dotted with grazing sheep and stone-built villages of fairy-tale charm. Jane Austen lived in nearby Bath for five years and likely walked these country lanes—the Jane Austen Centre is the city's biggest attraction and just a twenty-minute drive from camp. What would the reclusive author think of Campwell and its ethos of living a simpler, more natural life? In her own words: "To sit in the shade on a fine day and look upon verdure is the most perfect refreshment."

The Chief's Den includes a sundeck, a spacious living area, a bathroom, and its own kitchen with a wood-fired cast-iron stove.

A cool spot for hot yoga: The Cob Round is used as a gathering place for visitors.

OPPOSITE Campwell village guests prepare meals on the wood-fired cob oven and grills in the communal outdoor kitchen.

SKYCABIN

The SkyCabin, with its striking slanted roof, is a superstylish mid-century reboot of a vintage cabin in the sleepy small town of Skykomish, Washington, the gateway to the Alpine Lakes Wilderness. Handsome hardwood flooring replaced an old carpet in orange-red hues. Floor-to-ceiling windows open up the main room to the natural light, and a gas fireplace pumps out the heat. The main bedroom has big slanted windows with views onto the sun-dappled green woods. A modern kitchen is kitted out with a farmhouse sink and all the equipment you need for cooking and serving meals out on the big wooden deck, which has a round picnic table for communing under a towering fir. The thoughtful details add up: A French press and a fresh bag of Seattle's Best coffee await you in the kitchen, along with a dryer for your ski/snowboarding boots—you even can arrange for a massage therapist to come to the cabin for après-ski rubdowns.

The former mining and lumber town of Skykomish—the locals know it as Sky—sits in a scenic valley ringed by Cascades peaks and undeveloped forestland. In its early-twentieth-century heyday as a railroad hub, Sky was a stop for passenger trains with wanderlusty names like the Western Star, Empire Builder, and the Oriental Limited; the cabin is located near the train tracks, so you may hear the occasional lonesome whistle blow.

These days, the prevailing industry in Sky is outdoor recreation—and the opportunities for breathing in that fresh mountain air are boundless. Abandoned logging roads are now mountain-biking and snowmobiling trails. Stevens Pass has one of the top ski resorts in western Washington, with 1,125 acres (455 ha) of skiing and snowboarding terrain. The free-flowing Skykomish River offers 10 miles (16 km) of Class III–V white-water rapids and some gentler stretches for tubing and swimming, and the fly-fishing here is first-rate; the river is a natural spawning habitat for four types of Pacific salmon and steelhead trout.

Tucked into a nook, the kitchen is actually spacious enough to hold a farmhouse sink and a dishwasher.

OPPOSITE *The view from the loft showcases the airy living area and floor-to-ceiling windows.*

PLATBOS FOREST CABINS

Between the mountains and the sea on South Africa's Western Cape is a wild artifact from ancient times, a jewel of indigenous, old-growth forest known as platbos (Afrikaans for "flat forest or bush") that survived centuries of fires, storms, and lumbering. In the Platbos Forest, tree trunks are twisted and gnarled; branches stretch out like feathery fingers. The densely woven green canopy is dripping in old-man's beard and spidery ferns, forming a cool shelter for a biodiverse array of flora and fauna, from velvety mosses and lichens to baboons and Cape bushbucks. It's a landscape of almost primeval beauty.

The private Platbos Forest Reserve is also shelter to a handful of remarkable off-the-grid cabins, of which the two-person Bush Buck Suite is a standout: Built around a five-hundred-year-old white stinkwood tree, it has one long open side exposed to the forest (with drop-down blinds for privacy; there's also a mosquito net over the bed). Accommodations are rustic but comfy and full of charm, with a kitchenette and a woodstove and hot water available via a retro "donkey boiler

system." Solar lanterns and candles are provided; they give the three-sided cabin a honeyed glow.

The reserve is located in a valley that's a two-hour drive from Cape Town. Nearby are wineries, bike trails, and a rocky shoreline with sightings of southern right whales. Once you're settled in Platbos, though, you may not want to leave—the serenity of the forest is a potent force. A wooded trail over gentle terrain can be reached by private pathways from each cabin, with benches along the way for quiet contemplation. It's a two-hour stroll to the Canopy Lookout tower; take a climb for panoramic forest views. In spring, wildflowers push out of the forest floor.

One of the country's oldest milkwood survivors, said to be a thousand years old, is here. Milkwood was once a common hardwood in South Africa, but the forests were largely decimated by early colonizers. The gnarled milkwoods in Platbos are genetically one plant—when one collapses, new trees sprout from the trunks of the old. The reserve's conservation-minded owners offer guests a tree sapling to take home, and the ancient forest lives on.

WOODLAND CHASE TREEHOUSE

Northumberland, the northernmost county of England, was once the site of epic clashes for kingdoms. Today these bucolic grass hills are pocked with Iron Age forts and castle ruins. The British passion for the "gentle art of tramping" is alive and well here, with trekking paths meandering among wild meadows and ancient crags. It's a soulful place to explore, and ripe for countryside glamping. But not just any glamping: In historical Northumberland, vintage shepherd's huts and caravans have been retooled for fancified overnight stays. With its bespoke cabins, Woodland Chase just may outglamp them all.

Located on the family-owned Old Felton Farm, Woodland Chase is home to a menagerie of adorable animals, from white lambs and baby ducks to doe-eyed Velcro dogs. Each of the farm's three boutique glamping cabins has its own outdoor wood-fired hot tub and firepit; inside is a mix of elegant furnishings and handcrafted earthiness. Up on stilts and nestled in trees, the Treehouse is our pick of the bunch. It has fur-clad deck loungers crafted from aged whiskey barrels and a handmade wooden bed swathed in gazillion-thread-count Egyptian cotton. In the living area, a green velvet chesterfield and a William Morris rug share space with a country woodstove.

The windswept North Sea coastline is just a thirty-minute drive away. Be sure to check out the Northumberland coast's killer lineup of castles: J. M. W. Turner painted the ragtag battlements of Dunstanburgh; Warkworth was immortalized in Shakespeare's *Henry IV, Part I*; Bamburgh is a film-industry fave, as is the eleventh-century Alnwick Castle, which served as the exterior of Hogwarts in the first two Harry Potter movies. A scenic stretch of the two-thousand-year-old Hadrian's Wall, the legendary 73-mile-long (117 km) barrier built by the Romans, curves through Northumberland National Park. Closer to home, you can combine an easy footpath stroll with a pub crawl in the medieval village of Felton, a mile (1.6 km) away. After a good day's tramping, it's back to your glampsite.

The high-ceilinged cabin combines rustic touches like recycled farm materials with modern conveniences such as underfloor heating and electric blinds.

A twisty wooden staircase
strung with fairy lights
leads to the treehouse

GETAWAY

The Getaway is not one cabin but a whole truckload of them. These shoeboxlike retreats in beautiful, remote locations around the US provide an escape from urban living. So, for example, your Getaway escape from Los Angeles is one of forty rural cabins in the forested San Bernardino Mountains near Big Bear Lake, two hours north of the city. Each cabin is located 50 to 150 feet (15 to 46 m) away from its neighbor, providing a sense of solitude but not complete isolation.

As the company likes to say, Getaway cabins have everything you need and nothing you don't. The setting is the thing here, and each unit comes outfitted with a giant wall of a bedroom window and an outdoor firepit. The interiors are just 140 to 200 square feet (13 to 19 sq m) but pack a lot of comfort into the compact space, with a queen bed, private toilet and hot shower, and mini kitchen with all the cooking basics, like a

two-burner stovetop and a tiny fridge. The plush bed fits just so into the big window nook, perfect for snuggling up with a book. The cabins even have air-conditioning and heat. A cell phone lockbox encourages committed unplugging.

Locations are thoughtfully selected, and the Getaway website offers an impressive array of travel-planning guidance for each destination, including suggestions for hiking trails, local breweries, even nearby swimming holes. The Getaway escape from Washington, DC, for example, is close to Shenandoah National Park and its exceptional hiking, biking, and leaf-peeping opportunities. Between Austin and San Antonio, the Getaway cabins are located in Texas Hill Country, home to fields of blossoming bluebonnets and vineyards. Near Atlanta is Getaway Chattahoochee, where you stay near the North Georgia national forest of mountains, falls, and trout streams.

FARAWAY
TREEHOUSE

Cumbria, England

If there's one thing this cozy-cabin boom has shown, it's that you don't need a McMansion to live well, especially when the great outdoors is in your backyard. Canopy & Stars, a UK-based company with a highly curated collection of rental properties throughout Europe, figured all that out a while ago. Their specialty is finding unique, scaled-down dwellings in wild, gorgeous settings. Comfort and low-impact living are a given; a sense of whimsy, even better. Canopy & Stars' roster of singular rentals includes restored horse-drawn caravans, shepherd's huts, treehouses, tepees, yurts, sailing barges, and safari tents.

Case in point: the Faraway Treehouse, which feels as if it's been cobbled together by fairies. It marries rustic touches (plank floors, wooden walls) with the occasional pop of baroque, like a filigreed chandelier and dining chairs with ornately carved backs. Cubbyhole beds are plumped with velvety pillows and rich faux-fur throws, and a little woodstove painted robin's-egg blue hums with heat. Decorative teapots and twisted tree limbs give the interior a storybook feel.

The Faraway Treehouse sits up in the leafy canopy of a private 23-acre (9.3 ha) woodlands farm. You'll need your wellies to tramp the muddy woodlands and trails tracing the riverbank of the nearby River Lyne, plus your bathing suit for wild swimming.

From the treehouse, it's just a fifteen-minute drive to ancient Hadrian's Wall, a 73-mile-long (117 km) barrier built by the Romans in 122 CE, and a twenty-five-minute drive to Talkin Tarn, a glacial lake and park where you can rent kayaks and rowboats and hike short, easy trails that coil around the tarn among beech-trees and ancient oaks. Have a pub tipple in the nearby market town of Brampton, and finish the day with a warm chiminea fire outside the cabin, under a vivid night sky.

The cabin's quaint touches include a kitchen backsplash crafted of vintage crockery.

OPPOSITE *Oversize windows let in the surrounding woodlands.*

TYE RIVER CABIN CO.

Skykomish,
Washington State

This complex of three Cascade Range A-frames just an hour's drive from Seattle offers a master class in idyllic Pacific Northwest cabin living. Tye Haus and its sister cabins, Sky Haus and Foss Haus, are set in the Mount Baker–Snoqualmie National Forest, a misty, moody terrain of Douglas fir and western hemlock. These are A-frames with attitude: Foss Haus (pictured opposite) has a steep, slightly off-kilter pitch; the upstairs loft faces Beckler Peak. The triangle of Tye Haus is framed in strings of honey-hued lights, a deep-forest beacon welcoming you in from the cold. Sky Haus is smartly compact, a glass-and-wood model of stylish efficiency.

The owners bought Tye Haus as a ski cabin and gave it a thorough remodel; the rest is Instagram history. Both Tye Haus and Sky Haus come with outdoor hot tubs and firepits. Foss Haus includes a roomy bedroom downstairs. All feature toasty gas fireplaces and fully furnished kitchens and are part of the private cabin community of Timberlane Village, just outside of Skykomish.

One of the main appeals of the complex is its location: The convergence of outdoor activities in the area is simply mind-blowing. The cabins are close to hundreds of classic PNW hiking trails, including a forest trek to Bridal Veil Falls, which cascades down a rugged granite rock face. For ski bums, Stevens Pass is 10 miles (16 km) away; these are the closest cabins with electricity to the Cascades ski resort. The area averages 150 inches (381 cm) of snow each winter, and glacier-fed Lake Wenatchee nearby has marked snowshoe trails and 25 miles (40 km) of groomed cross-country-ski trails.

Summer adventures on Lake Wenatchee include windsurfing, white-water kayaking, and fishing for sockeye salmon. Trails from the cabin lead to a private community beach on the South Fork of the Skykomish River. TyeRiverCabinCo.com features a customized map with the best local hikes, activities, attractions, and restaurants; it also has a live webcam that lets you check road conditions before you head out.

Tye Haus is larger than it looks at 1,100 square feet (102 sq m), with a spacious living room and a lofted bedroom.

The Skykomish River rushes through the Cascade Range. Mount Index is visible in the background.

LOOKING GLASS TREEHOUSE

The kid outgrows the treehouse, but does the treehouse ever outgrow the kid? In the case of Django Kroner, a lifelong love for treehouses not only shadowed him into adulthood but also solidified his career path as a treehouse designer and craftsman. Kroner's builds aren't just for kids—they are beloved by families and couples craving more nature, more privacy, more off-the-grid living.

The Canopy Crew, Kroner's custom treehouse building and tree-care company, offers treehouse rentals in the sylvan forest canopy of Red River Gorge, Kentucky. The region is ripe for treehouse construction, with a deciduous forest of mighty maples and sweet gums and two-hundred-year-old oaks. Protecting the trees that hold the houses is an essential part of each build: "Trees are living, growing, moving beings," says Kroner, "so when we build in them, we design to fit each individual tree and put as little stress on it as possible."

The Canopy Crew's most ambitious project to date, the Looking Glass Treehouse, is situated high in the branches of a huge pignut hickory tree and a tulip poplar. Looking Glass is not one treehouse but two, connected by a bridge walkway. Only a long set of stairs from the forest floor is attached to the walkway; the octagonal houses practically float in the canopy. Chevron cutouts hold mirrors that reflect the changing colors of the forest. Looking Glass has plumbing and electricity to support a complete bathhouse and a fully stocked kitchen—the Crew ran the utilities up the staircase and across the bridge.

Most members of the high-flying Canopy Crew, Kroner included, are part of a rock-climbing community drawn to the world-class rock faces of eastern Kentucky. The Red River Gorge area in Kentucky's Daniel Boone National Forest boasts myriad scenic attractions: stone arches and sandstone cliffs, natural bridges, waterfalls, and overlooks. It's just 5 miles (8 km) from the treehouse to the Natural Bridge State Resort Park, with hiking, boating, swimming, caving, fishing, and, in the summertime, evening hoedowns, led by a professional square-dance caller.

THE LAZY DUCK

Inverness-shire,
Scotland

Its motto, "Come Home to Slow Living," expresses all that the Lazy Duck enterprise holds dear. Tucked into 6 acres (2.4 ha) of ancient pines and grassy meadows, each of the four Lazy Duck cabins has a slightly ramshackle rusticity, but inside is a feathered nest of old-fashioned comfort. You are invited to bike, hike, or tour the beautiful Scottish countryside, or just settle into a rocking chair and take your cue from the flocks of ducks and chickens that waddle about the grounds in giddy revelry, simply being.

Lazy Duck grew organically from its beginnings in 1999, when the original owners opened up their duck-keeper's cabin to visitors. Essentially a gussied-up chicken coop—with actual chickens pecking at the picket fence—the cabin (now called the Homestead) has a throwback interior of overstuffed armchairs, rockers, a woodstove, and vintage plates. From there, the Lazy Duck empire grew in higgledy-piggledy fashion into the four-cabin property it is now. The rustic Woodman's Hut (pictured opposite) is the most secluded, but all cabins come with small kitchens stocked with cooking essentials and indoor woodstoves;

rainwater bush showers; and composting toilets. Verandas have freestanding chimineas and bags of fragrant Macallan whisky-barrel-stave firewood to really light them up.

Yoga practitioners and massage therapists offer Swedish and acupressure spa treatments in the Well-Being Studio, which also has a six-person wood-fired hot tub built from Scandinavian larch, and an infrared sauna. Some thirty rare-breed ducks, including Aylesbury and goldeneye, call the property home, as does a small flock of Soay sheep from the St. Kilda archipelago. In spring, apple, cherry, and plum trees burst into blooming color.

The Lazy Duck puts you close to plenty of year-round outdoor activities. Nearby biking trails include a loop over the Pass of Ryvoan and another over the moorlands. Cairngorms National Park offers skiing, hiking, and mountain biking. The cabins are within walking distance of a network of cross-country-ski trails and right between the Cairngorms and Lecht ski areas. You can ice-climb in the Northern Corries or arrange water-sports adventures in Aviemore, a twenty-minute drive away.

Duck's Nest hangs on the lip of the duck pond for round-the-clock waterfowl viewing.

OPPOSITE *Firewood piled high behind the Duck's Nest is at the ready for chilly nights around the porch chiminea.*

TWIN PINES CHALET

Despite all its straight lines and right angles, this cabin has a thing for curves—mid-century modern curves, to be exact. In the living room, round stools and a sculptural walnut-and-glass Isamu Noguchi coffee table face a vintage Adrian Pearsall gondola sofa with undulating lines. A marble tulip dining table is paired with shapely mid-century-style chairs and a cord pendant light. Even the room's big mirror has rounded edges. Needless to say, this is not your average rustic retreat.

Twin Pines is named for the two tall pines that stand sentry at the cabin's front. A sturdy relic from 1966, the little red-cedar chalet is shaded all around by towering pines. It's just plain adorable, with diamond-pane windows and a cheerful moss-green trim. Inside, the abundant flea-market scores include that curvy mid-century sofa, now claiming pride of place next to a big brick wood-burning fireplace. The cabin is surprisingly roomy, with a high-pitched ceiling in the living area, an enormous bedroom loft, and a galley kitchen. Original kitchen cabinets were given new life with a good sanding and a lovely blue paint job; a local craftsman made identical cabinets for the galley kitchen's opposite side. A matte-black sink and quartzite countertops add even more pizzazz. The downstairs bedroom is a snug nest, with a modern Thuma bed frame and a wood-paneled wall painted a deeply saturated blue. Two mid-century lighting fixtures in red add a pop of bright color.

A spacious outdoor deck, with a gas grill and red Adirondack-style chairs, is a sun-dappled haven for hanging out. Twin Pines is located in a friendly "neighborhood" of cabins, with close access to plenty of trails and Big Bear scenery. The Rose Hill Trailhead, just steps from the cabin, leads to two marked (and uncrowded) hiking trails. Around 6 miles (9.7 km) away is Boulder Bay Park, where you can take a dip in the brisk waters or do a little kayaking, and you're just minutes from the ski slopes and snowboard terrain of Big Bear Mountain Resort.

Fitting for this classic 1960s-era A-frame, the interior decorating scheme is mid-century, from the iconic Noguchi glass table to the curvy gondola sofa.

TREELOFT

This treehouse for two nestles in the bosky green canopy of Missouri forestland. Custom built and smart looking, it's elevated in a sylvan pocket of quiet and seclusion on BaseCamp at CedarFork, a 120-acre (49 ha) family farm. The TreeLoft puts a big emphasis on creature comforts—in the cozy furnishings, the gas fireplace, the hot-water shower, even air-conditioning—but it also provides a clean break from the digital rat race. In other words, you forgo Wi-Fi, cell-phone service, and TV in favor of the gentle cadences of heartland wilderness.

The TreeLoft is more or less one big, high-ceilinged room. A huge wall of windows overlooking the woods is its centerpiece. A king bed and seating face the windows, meaning you wake up in an outdoors state of mind. A deck off the living room lets you lounge in the sun-speckled tree canopy; another deck has a hot tub shaded by eastern red cedars. Log seats and twinkle lights ring a firepit below.

This region of Missouri is all about the deep woods—and wine. When you stay at TreeLoft, you're just a fifteen- to thirty-minute drive from a charmingly diverse array of wineries and breweries. Family-owned Apple Creek is an estate winery making everything from a crisp Seyval Blanc to a semisweet rosé. Another family-run enterprise, Charleville, is both winery and microbrewery, where grapevines embroider the rolling contours of Missouri hills.

Missouri is also Mark Twain country. The author was born in the tiny settlement of Florida, Missouri, and despite spending his adult years elsewhere, Twain claimed he would always be "a border ruffian from the State of Missouri." Ninety minutes from the TreeLoft by car is the Mark Twain National Forest, with 750 miles (1,207 km) of hiking and mountain-bike trails. You're also just a twenty-minute drive from the Mississippi River, where young Twain was a riverboat pilot, a job requiring that he "get up a warm personal acquaintanceship with every old snag and one-limbed cottonwood . . . for 1,200 miles." The wild spirit of Huck Finn is not only out on the riverfront but also up in the canopy in TreeLoft's Missouri woods.

The appliances in the stylish kitchen are scaled down to fit the compact space.

OPPOSITE The massive cabin window lets guests enjoy uncluttered Missouri forest views from any angle.

KNOWLTON AND CO. TREEHOUSE

This is the story of a little tree fort in the forest wilds of Ontario. It grew so handsomely and became so wonderful that it's now one of the top vacation rentals not just in Canada but in the world. It's the work of interior designer Lynne Knowlton. She and her husband, Michael, turned what started as a children's tree fort into a boutique glamping retreat, complete with treehouse, cabin, pool, and outdoor kitchen, all on the couple's 100-acre (40 ha) rural property.

The fort was originally built for the Knowltons' four children in a thicket of tangled woods that the kids called the "witches' forest." It's still a forest: Only six trees were trimmed in the process of building the structure. The reclaimed materials used to build the fort read like a catalog of wrecking-ball odds and ends: Walls and floors were salvaged from an old barn; one wall was crafted from the barn's tin roof. Windows (one stained-glass) were rescued from a church set to be demolished. The decorative spindles in the teak deck railings were spotted rusting in a pile at a yard sale.

The alfresco dining table and chairs—complete with the odd bruise and splash of old paint—were fashioned from reclaimed wooden boats. They now claim pride of place under the treehouse.

Turns out, the adults loved the little tree fort as much as the kids, so Lynne and her daughter Tristan went to work turning the rough interior into a homey, ultrastylish (tree)house. The theme is variations on white: The dark-wood walls and floors were brightened by warm white paint, and linens and furnishings in shades of white and neutrals lit up the place even more. Textured fibers were paired with natural materials, like a braided jute rug on the reclaimed wood floor. The devil is in the precisely edited details, like a carved stone sink from Bali and pretty patterned outdoor lanterns. A roaring woodstove makes the ground-floor patio a go-to space, and hammock chairs and wicker balcony swings add to the sense of play—as does the awesome slide that can be used in lieu of the stairs. When you're not swinging in your treehouse, get walking: The property has 100 miles (161 km) of wooded country trails.

GREY DUCK CABIN

If you've got a yen for backcountry living but an allergy to roughing it, this Northwoods cabin should more than satisfy it. Grey Duck Cabin is seriously comfortable, loaded with modern conveniences (Wi-Fi, in-floor heating), and beautiful to boot. It sits on 40 acres (16 ha) of secluded forest and state parkland. Private trails lead to the Manitou River, which snakes through the evergreen terrain in summer and freezes into photogenic ice sculptures in winter. You can tramp through stands of towering firs, fish for brook and rainbow trout, or simply hunker down in the serene comfort of your cabin. A sun-splashed open-plan living area showcases the outdoors with 14-foot (4.3 m) floor-to-ceiling windows. A cedar screened porch open on three sides puts you into a woodland soundscape all year round.

The Grey Duck is off the grid, reliant on solar energy backed by a generator if you need it. For extra warmth, the living area has a radiant gas fireplace. A telescope in front of the floor-to-ceiling window lets you zoom in on the glittering Milky Way. On-trend design elements in the handsome kitchen include a subway-tile backsplash and concrete countertops. If you don't feel like cooking, the town of Finland is a short drive away and has a co-op general store and a handful of restaurants.

Snowed in? Four sets of snowshoes are provided to get you out onto the white stuff. The cabin is also close to the C.J. Ramstad Trail, which runs from Duluth to Grand Marais and is perfect for snowmobiling in winter or hiking and horseback riding in the warmer months. (It snows a whole lot up here in the North Shore backcountry, and the owners recommend that guests rent an AWD or 4WD vehicle for winter stays.) In summer, the landscape transforms into endless fields of purple and pink lupines; keep your eyes peeled for the occasional moose. A rocky 7-mile (11 km) round-trip hike to Bean and Bear Lakes rewards with scenic lake overlooks. Other nearby outdoor pleasures include skiing (in the Lutsen Mountains), kayaking tours exploring Lake Superior caves, and wilderness canoeing.

The house lies on 40 acres (16 ha) of private wilderness in Minnesota's snowy North Shore backcountry.

Built in 2019, the custom-designed Grey Duck is off the grid but stocked with modern conveniences like in-floor heating.

LITTLE OWL CABIN

Little Owl meets the rustic-chic Pacific Northwest aesthetic right where it lives. Cedar soaking tubs beneath towering conifers? Check. State-of-the-art coffee-making machinery, including an adjustable burr coffee grinder? Check, check. A sylvan setting just a twenty-minute drive to Mount Rainier National Park and the White Pass Ski Area, and smack-dab in the middle of the Gifford Pinchot National Forest? Yes—and happy trails to you.

Wilderness is all around, but creature comforts rule the cabin. A gorgeous remodel of a 1965 A-frame has made the Little Owl one of the most well-appointed rentals in the Mount Rainier region. The twice-yearly Packwood Flea Market is the source for several of the home's vintage adornments, including a red dhurrie rug in the living area. The sun-drenched loft has a large triangle of a window that looks out on dense forestland of leggy conifers, and steps from the cabin's back door is a hammock strung in the trees for a little meditative swaying.

Despite the cozily outfitted interior, the outdoors has an irresistible pull here. You're close to meadows of alpine wildflowers and powder-packed ski slopes (the area gets more than 400 inches/10 m of snow yearly). In early summer, rhododendrons bloom in a dreamscape of sword ferns and firs. The trail to Packwood Lake is an easy twenty-minute stroll, while the trailhead for a hiking path up Tatoosh Peak is right on the property line.

You're also close to the Mount Fremont Lookout, a 1934 former fire lookout atop a 7,000-foot (2,134 m) rocky knoll, with expansive views of Rainier and the Cascades. The trail crosses meadowland and steep crags, home to a herd of mountain goats. The White Pass ski resort, with uncrowded acreage for powder skiing and snowboarding, is a half-hour drive away. In late summer and fall, you can hunt for chanterelle mushrooms in nearby woods—or forage for a hazy IPA at the Packwood Brewing Co., which is housed in a handsomely restored dollar store from 1933.

PARC OMEGA

A wolf's howl is a spine-tingling, almost primeval sound. Spend the night in one of the wolf cabins in Parc Omega, a 2,200-acre (890 ha) wildlife park in the Outaouais region of Quebec, and you can experience the calls of a wolf pack up close.

These handsome log cabins are outfitted for modern comfort, with full kitchens and cozy beds draped in colorful wool blankets. Large windows of triple-glazed glass overlook the wolf enclosure for panoramic viewing—you can actually sit nose-to-nose with one of the pack. But the wolves, lying contentedly in the snow outside the glass, give you the sense that it's the humans who are on display here, relegated as you are to the confines of your cabin habitat. Then night falls, the wolves raise their heads to the sky and howl, and you're back in the wild.

The star of Parc Omega's wolf accommodations is perhaps the Wolf Lodge, with a roomy 1,362 square feet (127 sq m) of living space. It can sleep up to six guests, and features soaring ceilings, mezzanine lofts, and massive bay windows for prime wolf viewing. The lodge and its sister properties, the Wolf Cabin and Wolf Chalet, are the latest innovations at the Quebec park, which is home to a thriving population of North American wildlife, including bison, black and cinnamon bears, reindeer, caribou, elk, musk oxen, wild turkeys, and ibex. The park's wolf packs include black and arctic wolves, but the pride of Parc Omega is the gray wolf, aka the timber wolf, whose numbers have been decimated in recent decades by hunting and habitat destruction.

The park is open year-round for self-drive safaris on a 6.8-mile (11 km) car trail, where you can photograph wildlife and roll down your window here and there to feed a carrot to a laid-back deer. You're allowed out of your vehicle only in designated walking-trail zones and in the Land of the Pioneers, which has a gray wolf observatory and a restored farm with pettable animals. You can also walk (or snowshoe) the First Nations Trail, which is lined with hand-carved totems by local Algonquian artist Denis Charette. Among the distinctively Canadian experiences at Parc Omega is a visit to the *cabane à sucre* (sugar shack), where workers make maple-sugar taffy outdoors from mid-February to the end of March. Hot maple sugar is drizzled on snow and in minutes turns to chewy taffy, another taste of the wild in a park full of them.

The wolves are literally at your door (well, window) when you stay in one of Parc Omega's comfy wolf cabins.

THE HUNTER GREENHOUSE

When Ely and Danielle Franko bought a mess of a flat-roofed A-frame on 3 acres (1.2 ha) of Catskills woods in 2016, they were inexperienced in pretty much all aspects of home renovation. Two years later, they were winning design awards, and the cabin had become an Airbnb favorite.

This self-taught duo did the labor themselves, demoing the dated innards of the 1971 cabin and starting from scratch. They pulled up vinyl flooring to discover virgin hardwood, and rescued water-damaged walls with several coats of Benjamin Moore White Dove paint. They removed Formica "wood" paneling, and KO'd a pink kitchen countertop. They even constructed some of their own furniture: They wanted to make a dining room table out of reclaimed wood, but it was out of their price range, so they bought some boards of Douglas fir from a lumberyard and bashed the wood with rocks to give it a weathered look. The built-in seating against the wall is also a Franko custom build, as is the long outdoor farm table, which is lit by strands of Edison bulbs hung from the trees.

The Greenhouse grounds back up to protected state land ideal for deep backwoods walks. The owners had no idea when they bought the property that just down the street—literally—are two of the Catskills' biggest attractions: North-South Lake, a scenic spot for hiking, boating, and swimming in the Catskill Forest Preserve, and Kaaterskill Falls, a splendid two-tiered waterfall. The cabin is also just a fifteen-minute drive from Hunter Mountain and its popular ski center—even if you don't ski, you can take in the heights on the six-passenger chairlifts of the Hunter Mountain Scenic Skyride.

The Greenhouse now has a sibling, the Barnhouse, the owners' fabulous conversion of an 1845 hay barn in Jewett, New York. Among other things, it has a rope swing hung from rustic beams in front of a wood-burning fireplace and features Fireclay tiles in hues of sand, feldspar, and mustard.

At the top of the stairs is a sunny sitting area with a hanging chair and a pillow-filled reading nook.

OPPOSITE *The Greenhouse is aptly named: It's home to some fifty plants, including a 16-foot (4.9 m) wall of green gracing the open-plan living area.*

The Greenhouse's deck is one of the coziest spots on the property thanks to its roaring wood-burning chiminea and twinkling lights strung between trees.

OPPOSITE A 16-foot (5 m) double bank of windows in the living area shows off the cabin's outdoor space, complete with gazebo and custom-built farm table.

FERN GULLY CABINS

Sleep, play, and leave your cares behind at this sweet little retreat in the middle of a Vancouver Island rain forest. Fern Gully's creekside complex of three redwood cabins lies in the shadow of leggy firs, spruces, and cedars. This is quintessential Pacific Northwest: You'll be walking mist-shrouded paths lined with ferns, beachcombing at nearby ocean strands, and falling asleep to the happy burble of creek song.

The Fern Gully complex has a homegrown feel. Signs are charmingly handmade, and the path to the outhouse is strung with fairy lights. Located in a quiet cul-de-sac, the cabins share a tiny-house compactness, without a bit of wasted space. They are furnished modestly but contain all you need: futons, woodstoves, and scaled-down kitchens with mini fridges, single-burner stovetops, and sinks. The warm wood interiors may be snug, but big glass windows make the rain forest into an extension of the space—this is more glamping than backcountry basic. Outdoor showers offer a memorable rain-forest cleanse in the buff, and firepits warm you right up on cool nights. The place even smells great; you'll want to bottle up all that sweet fir perfume.

The cabins are within easy reach of gorgeous trails for hikers of all abilities. A scenic fifteen-minute hike through evergreen rain forest takes you to China Beach, a strand of tawny sand lapped by the steel-gray waves of the Pacific. Winter storms churn up the occasional surf break, but in summer, the sea rolls in with a glassy calm. In spring and fall, scan the horizon for whales and seals or beachcomb for polished stones and driftwood.

Thanks to its temperate climate, Vancouver Island's west coast is a great escape any time of year. And escape you will: No cell phone or internet service at Fern Gully means a clean break from the digital world. Now, *that's* how you unplug and unwind, Pacific Northwest–style.

Grand Fir
Cabin

WHISKEY CREEK CABIN

If the cabin of your dreams includes (1) a soulful forest setting right by a waterfall pond and wooded hiking trails; (2) a wraparound deck and a wall of windows to soak in the outdoors; and (3) stylish indoor comfort built into every nook and cranny, including a big ole roaring fireplace—then Whiskey Creek is your sweet cabin home. Oh, and it's just a ten-minute walk from civilization (and a brewery!).

Whiskey Creek Cabin is set in the heart of Mount San Jacinto State Park and the San Jacinto Wilderness, a high-altitude escape from the desert heat in nearby Palm Springs. It's a hiker's haven, with well-maintained forest trails climbing 10,834-foot (3,302 m) Mount San Jacinto, the second-highest peak in SoCal. The multilevel cabin is enveloped in tall pines and right next to an orchard of mature apple, pear, and plum trees. A pond attracts deer and other wildlife. You'll get a panoramic view from the upper-level deck, while hanging macramé swings on the lower deck put you a stone's throw from the cool pond and the glistening green forest. A garden illuminated by string lights holds the "Gathering Place," a seated area with a pine-straw floor, an ideal perch for spotting shooting stars.

Inside, the mid-century modern cabin has a fully stocked kitchen and two comfortable bedrooms, each with its own full bath. When the day of strolling wilderness trails is done, indoor pleasures include a big selection of books and games and a record player with a box full of vinyl. But this sylvan setting is so bewitching it may inspire you to pen a song instead—luckily, there's a guitar, piano, and didgeridoo on hand for impromptu musical noodling.

RIGHT *Make some noise:
Guests have the use of the
cabin's piano, guitar, and
didgeridoo for impromptu
jam sessions.*

BELOW *The interior mixes
mid-century furnishings with
bold-patterned rugs and
wallpaper and whimsical
touches like a wagon-wheel
chandelier lit with Edison
bulbs.*

The top-level wraparound deck is shaded by tall pines; below are a pond and a fruit orchard.

HERGEST LEE CABIN

In 2019, Welsh woodworker Paul Gent fell hard for rural Herefordshire, Wales, and its patchwork-quilt terrain of rolling grasslands. The area's centuries-old stone and timber-frame barns are so full of character that converting them into modern living spaces is practically a cottage industry. Gent soon found his own barn in the tiny hamlet of Burlingjobb, and he set about building a rental cabin on the property to raise funds for the barn conversion.

With only himself as the client, Gent was freed from design constraints. In lieu of a pitched roof or an A-frame, he gave the cabin a gently rounded apex. The roofline curves are mirrored in the interior walls; high ceilings and oversize windows add space and airiness. The elegantly compact kitchen has space-saving stackable stools and a hinged dining table. Inside the comfy bedroom is a freestanding bathtub perched right in front of an enormous picture window overlooking nearby Hanter Hill and Hergest Ridge. The redwood bed frames and shower washstand were crafted by Gent; the open living area features some of his paintings.

A fantastic floating wood staircase leads up to the little mezzanine (which sleeps three), with views of horse meadows and hills. Outside is a deck with a grill and a garden where you can watch the flitting of falcons and swifts. The firepit is a draw on chilly Welsh nights.

The area has no lack of scenic walks, aka "rambles," a number of which are close to the cabin's doorstep. The nearest village, Kington, is just a ten-minute drive away and is a popular center for rambling. (Look for the official acorn symbols denoting a national trail.) Also nearby are the Cider Circuit bike trails, where you can leisurely cycle from one apple farm and cider pub to the next. Pubs are an essential part of the landscape; hang around for a few days, and the Harp will fast become your favorite local haunt. Voted Country Pub of the Year in 2020, it's just a fifteen-minute walk from the Hergest Lee; the hearty fare includes roast sirloin of Hereford and fresh-battered Cornish cod. Pub and grub it, then walk off your meal on a lovely Welsh ramble.

LIVE OAK TREEHOUSE

The stars shine big and bright in the Texas nights at HoneyTree Farm and its winsome collection of five romantic treehouses. You'll wake up in the trees to the trills of Texas songbirds, listen to armadillos rustling down below, and fast become steeped in the restorative serenity of HoneyTree's 10 acres (4 ha) of Hill Country woods. Each treehouse is its own secluded space, and all are smartly outfitted in rustic-modern fashion. Big decks overlook the Palo Alto Creek, which flows lazily past the treehouses. "The creek provides a nice sparkle, a gurgle—and attracts all kinds of amazing wildlife," says Jacob Rhodes, who with his wife, Katie, designed and built the HoneyTree cabins. In summer, guests can splash in the shallow spring-fed creek.

HoneyTree's signature cabin might just be Live Oak, where the trunks of oak trees stretch toward the sky through cutouts in the deck. The interior features the cutest little tongue-and-groove Hobbit hole for curling up with a book and contemplating the leafy canopy outside. In the bedroom, polished pine beams and floors frame whitewashed walls, crisp white organic bed linens, and gossamer netting. Under the house is an outdoor tiled patio and candlelit soaking tub.

Guests can explore the HoneyTree woods on a tended loop trail frequented by wild turkeys, white-tailed deer, and armadillos. You're also just a ten-minute drive to Main Street in Fredericksburg. The town is the center of the Hill Country wine scene and home to some fifty wineries; folks come from all over for regional winery tours.

Fredericksburg is a great base for exploring the rolling Hill Country landscape, famed for its seasonal blush of bluebonnets and Indian paintbrush. In spring and summer, take a drive along Highway 16 on the 13-mile (21 km) stretch north to Willow City for peak wildflower viewing. And LBJ country is just down the road; you can visit the cabin of the former president's cattle-driving grandpappy, the white clapboard house of his youth, and his own sprawling cattle ranch, aka the Texas White House, at the Lyndon B. Johnson National Historical Park.

The deck of the Live Oak cabin was built around the trunks of the property's venerable oak trees.

OPPOSITE *Live Oak's board-and-batten exterior was painted a crab-apple green and topped with a metal roof.*

The industrial-size glass-paneled garage door (scavenged from a defunct elementary school building) opens up to the deck for indoor-outdoor living.

TINY CATSKILL CABIN

Kerhonkson,
New York

This tiny-indeed cabin unpacks in all sorts of interesting ways—so much so that it can sleep up to six people in its compact 500 square feet (46 sq m). Every little nook has some kind of utility: A queen bed is tucked into a snug corner in the loft; an office space has a full desk and its own window. There's even a washer-dryer. The kitchen is dollhouse compact (narrow range, half-size fridge), but it's a powerhouse, with handsome cherrywood cabinets stocked with every imaginable culinary tool. The biggest room in the cabin is the screened-in front porch, where you can warm yourself by a gas fireplace against a wall of cedar shingles. The three-season porch is strung with twinkling globe lights, for even more of that witchy Catskills magic.

Outside is all rough-hewn cedar shake and dense Kerhonkson woods; inside is twenty-first-century comfort and convenience, with Sonos speakers and good Wi-Fi, piles of stacked firewood, soft blankets, and textured pillows. S'mores fixin's are in the kitchen. Macramé hangs on the white walls. The bathroom is roomy, with a full tub and shower.

The Tiny Catskill Cabin may be tiny, but the 1-acre (0.4 ha) property offers plenty of outdoor space for stretching your legs and spending time in nature—plus it's got some 160 acres (65 ha) of private forest for a backyard. Dine out on the retro patio table and chairs or kick back on wood planks circling a blazing campfire. A hammock swings beneath the pines. Frequent visitors include deer, hawks, and scurrying chipmunks.

The cabin also makes a great base camp for adventure expeditions into the Catskills. It's just a twenty-minute drive to Lake Minnewaska for leafy hikes. One 6.8-mile (11 km) hike takes you to the tumbling falls of Awosting. Head into the classic hipster mountain towns of New Paltz and Woodstock when you need to forage for good food and drink, or climb the Gunks—the Shawangunk Mountains, that is—with classic rock-climbing walls and waterfall trails.

STONE CITY TREEHOUSE

If you're looking for the Vermont of picture postcards, the Northeast Kingdom is happy to oblige, with back roads coiled around mossy forests, pockets of shimmering lakes and ponds, and sweet little towns with white steeples and village greens. Deep in the woods of the Northeast Kingdom, near the small town of Hardwick, this gem of a treehouse is filled with loving touches.

It's a well-built tiny cottage with rustic charm (including vintage windows, sourced from an old schoolhouse). The living area is cozy, with an Oriental rug, a leather loveseat, and rows of books. A ladder leads to a bed in a just-big-enough loft with windows open to the gurgling stream outside. Outfitted with vintage wicker chairs and twinkling fairy lights, a deck out back overlooking the stream is a perfect perch for spotting critters. A sitting area, hammock, and campfire space just below the treehouse are right by the water.

You are still staying in a tiny treehouse, however, with limited space and amenities; there's a primitive composting toilet and no hot water (you have the option of using the modern bathroom in the main house), and electricity is fully solar powered. Cooking is done on a propane camping stove in the miniature kitchen, on the charcoal grill under the house, or by campfire near the rock-strewn stream. Or just don't cook at all. The village of Hardwick, 3 miles (4.8 km) away, is stocked with delis, bistros, pizza joints, and ice-cream shops. Hophead alert: Breweries are abundant in this corner of Vermont, from Lost Nation in Morrisville to Hill Farmstead in nearby Greensboro and Alchemist in Stowe.

Stowe isn't famous only for its brews—its celebrated mountain ski resort is just a twenty-minute drive away. But you don't have to go even that far afield to get out into the wild: Nichols Pond is a mile (1.6 km) away, and the cottage has kayaks for paddling (no motorized boats are allowed on this pretty reservoir). In summer, climb to Nichols Ledge for stunning views and listen to the night calls of owls and loons. In winter, strap on the house snowshoes for a hike, or take a cross-country-ski trek on the snowmobile trail (skis provided).

Many Stone City guests like to cook their meals over the campfire by the stream.

OPPOSITE *What the treehouse lacks in space, it makes up for in cozy charm, with two comfy armchairs and an Oriental rug.*

Our Jungle House,
page 131

2

Tropics

PHOENIX HOUSE

Pahōa, Big Island, Hawaii

Perched atop an ebony lava flat made by an eruption from the Kīlauea volcano in 1990, this 450-square-foot (42 sq m) "modern beach farmhouse" sits in the shadows of Mauna Loa. It's the work of the award-winning design team from ArtisTree, which builds sustainable houses using regenerative power, recycled materials, and biomimicry. The two-story Phoenix House is off-grid (with solar-powered electricity and a rainwater catchment system) but extremely comfy, with rustic, artful touches like vintage French doors and a tin-tub kitchen sink. The loft bedroom has ocean views and a splashy mural.

The thirty-year-old lava surrounding the house has hardened into gleaming undulations that in the day's shifting light can look like inky ocean waters. It's no wonder the Phoenix House, with its rusted exterior of corrugated metal and wide windows to take in the red-sky sunsets and sweeping breezes, makes you feel like you've set sail on a mad black sea.

The largest of the Hawaiian Islands, the Big Island has an almost breathtaking biodiversity. One minute you're sunbathing with sea turtles on a balmy beach; the next you're riding horses in lush Waipio Valley pastureland. You can climb to the top of Mauna Kea, the world's tallest mountain when measured from seafloor to peak. Or you can stare into the flaming caldera of an active volcano: The Kilauea volcano in Hawaii Volcanoes National Park has been belching fire and lighting up the night for nearly forty years. Closer to Phoenix House, the Kalapana viewing area is just a four-mile (6.4 km) bike ride away—if you're lucky, you'll see gold and orange ribbons of molten magma swirling into the sea with a magnificent hiss.

The cycle of life on the Big Island operates on both a macro and micro scale. The native Hawaiian tree known as the ohia, for example, is often the first tree to sprout on the scene of a fresh lava flow, the little red blooms making their way out of the blackness. Like the aptly named Phoenix House, it's a vivid example of beauty rising from the ashes.

The solidified lava flats
that surround the house
are from the 1990 eruption
of the Kilauea volcano.

CASA ALICE

This wood chalet perched on the hilltop of a Puerto Rican rain forest is a striking sight thanks to its electrifying blue roof, deck, and trim. Tropical color reigns inside as well as out, from saffron walls in the warm, wood-beamed living room to the green tile countertops and gleaming wood cabinets in the fabulous kitchen. The rich, deeply saturated colors of the house echo the vividness of the Caribbean Sea, visible from both upper and lower decks.

This artsy, sun-strewn three-bedroom chalet has plenty of vintage charm, but the tasteful furnishings and cool artwork elevate the look. Modern upgrades include air-conditioning and a contemporary cook's kitchen with stainless-steel appliances. Louvered windows roll up and down to let in balmy breezes and the sound of the coqui frogs singing through the night.

The cabin lies twenty-five minutes by car from Old San Juan, on the wild fringes of El Yunque National Forest, the only tropical rain forest in the US Forest Service system. This largely untrammeled terrain has a Jurassic Park feel (sans the dinos),

dense with palm forests, giant ferns, and a coterie of colorful birds and hothouse blooms. A drive on Route 191 takes you past scenic overlooks, peaks, and waterfalls, and you may run into a light rain shower or two; every year, the forest gets 200 inches (5.1 m) of rain.

Or head out to the coast to while away the day on the palm-shaded beauty of a Puerto Rican beach. The chalet is just ten minutes by car from the sugary white sand and tranquil seas at Luquillo Beach, with kiosks nearby selling local food and spirits. Or drive fifteen minutes farther to Fajardo, where water taxis wait to deliver you to gorgeous cays like Cayo Icacos for snorkeling and swimming. Also in Fajardo is one of the country's unique attractions: a bioluminescent bay. The evening waters in Las Croabas Lagoon literally shimmer from the light of tiny organisms called dinoflagellates that glow in response to the wave of a hand or the dip of a paddle. Several companies in Farjardo offer bio bay kayak tours, so pick a cloudy, moonless night for a cool dip into liquid starlight.

HIDEOUT BALI

Selat, Bali,
Indonesia

When it comes to ultraromantic retreats, Bali has it all going on. But the Hideout will leave even the most seasoned traveler breathless. With its five honeycomb bamboo huts perched high in the misty mountains of the Gunung Agung volcano, this seductive eco-retreat takes you off the grid and straight into a reverie. It's not called "Hideout" for nothing: You're far off the tourist path, cradled in a tangle of jungle green. Solitude is broken only by the music of rippling river waters below and the occasional nudge of the Hideout's friendly house dogs and cats. The sublime setting provides a matchless sense of peace and tranquility.

Explore the area by scooter or hire a driver to show you the highlights. You're just minutes away from a sunrise trek up Mount Agung, Bali's highest and most sacred mountain, rising 10,308 feet (3,142 m) above carpets of rice paddies. While you're there, pay your respects to the gods at the ancient temple complex of Pura Besakih, which somehow survived unscathed when a volcanic eruption blew the top off Mount Agung in 1963. At the cinematic jungle waterfall known as Air Terjun Jagasatru, you can swim in a rock-strewn pool beneath the falls. The nearest local beach, Padang Padang, a forty-minute scooter ride away, is epic, all sugary sand and frothy jade seas.

Each of the five Hideout cabins is an architectural marvel, crafted entirely of bamboo, from the stairs to the floors to the tables and chairs; even the sheets are made from bamboo fibers. Bamboo beds are fitted with plump mattresses and silk netting. The houses are two-tiered, with floor-to-ceiling A-frame windows in the second-level bedroom. All are lit from within by sexy Balinese lamps that cast an amber glow. The open-air houses have no doors, no air-conditioning, just the cool kiss of mountain air, and each comes with its own outdoor shower and lush garden of massive ferns.

Balinese hospitality is legendary, and Hideout is no exception: In-room massages are a must, and freshly cooked meals are delivered to your bungalow daily by the friendly staff. You awaken to banana pancakes and fresh Balinese coffee. Dusk arrives with a soft sparkle of fireflies along the river and a blue-black sky swirling with stars. This is paradise, all right—a reverie come to life.

The valleys surrounding Mount Agung are filled with lush rice paddies.

At Hideout Horizon, one of Hideout Bali's five unique jungle retreats, a bamboo ramp leads to netting overlooking an indoor-outdoor plunge pool.

OUR JUNGLE HOUSE

Surat Thani,
Thailand

Our Jungle House is an eco-resort pioneer, welcoming guests to its 25 acres (10 ha) of private Thai rain forest for more than thirty years. Their cluster of twenty-one rustic hardwood treehouses and bungalows lies at the entrance to Khao Sok National Park and its ancient evergreen forest.

This is not just the ideal place for a serious relaxation reset, it's also a baptism in hothouse green. You'll swim in sparkling river water lined by sheer white cliffs of weathered stone. Sunset cocktails on the rooftop bar will arrive wrapped in voluptuous jungle flowers. And you'll end the day falling asleep to the kiss of balmy breezes and a choir of rain-forest chatter.

Our Jungle House cabins gaze out over river streams and limestone cliffs bearded in green foliage, and no two are alike. The Half Moon treehouse (pictured opposite) has cliffside views and room enough for a family of four; the Nature bungalow sits on the cool jungle floor swathed in ferns and wild banana trees. Cabin exteriors are crafted of sturdy hardwoods, while interiors have delicate touches, like woven bamboo walls and carved wooden doors. Upscale comforts include beds of soft linens (and mosquito netting) and hot showers with lemongrass soaps. There's no air-conditioning, but fans keep the cool night air circulating. The exceptionally fresh organic meals include red and green Thai curries and just-squeezed fruit juices.

Three nature trails meander the resort past oversize ferns and palms; look for hornbills, monkeys, civet cats, and the rarely seen slow loris. (And yes, snakes and insects—the jungle is pristine, but it hasn't been sanitized for risk-free living.) When the rivers are at high levels, tubing the rushing water is super fun. Our Jungle House is just over a half mile (805 m) from the town of Khao Sok, an easy stroll to pick up groceries or shop. The resort also offers a fabulous selection of tours exploring the mountains and lakes of Khao Sok National Park. You can ride a bamboo raft on the Khlong Sok river, explore secret caves in deep forest, and see wild Asian elephants. Or simply relax in your room and enjoy the pampering of a Thai massage.

The Half Moon cabin treehouse has spectacular river views and is located along the daily route of the property's monkeys.

TRIANGLE SIARGAO

The little A-frame in the woods has hitched a ride to the tropics. Set in a garden of dewy ferns and coconut palms, this beautiful open-air bungalow in the Philippines municipality of General Luna on Siargao Island has a lush setting and a bohemian spirit. It has all the creature comforts—fully equipped kitchen, modern bathrooms, custom furnishings—except air-conditioning. But you won't miss it, as windows throughout the cabin flip open to wafting jungle garden scents, and ceiling fans keep the balmy breezes flowing. A Filipino-style *nipa* (thatched) roof runs all the way to the ground and stretches forward to shade the patio.

The 753-square-foot (70 sq m) bungalow has a high-ceilinged living area with a cushioned platform sofa and chairs and a dining table. A tree swing in the middle of the room is something to haggle over. Upstairs in the mezzanine, a spacious bedroom lies behind long white curtains and a custom loveseat overlooks the garden. Out back is a little herb garden for your harvesting pleasure, and the owners' three adorable dogs are forever bopping somewhere in the yard.

Siargao is an island of virgin jungle, coconut farms, mangrove forests, and big-time surfable waves. Cloud 9 beach, just minutes from the bungalow, has the island's most celebrated surf break. Typhoon swells roil up tubular Pacific waves from August to early November, but Cloud 9's barreling right-handers are good any time of year.

For a relaxed beach hang, take a thirty-minute ride on a *habal-habal* (modified motorbike) through jungle and rice fields to Magpupungko Beach. At low tide, the frothy Pacific recedes, and clear turquoise pools emerge amid natural rock formations—slip in for a refreshing swim. The powdery blond beach has snack stands where you can sip a *buko* juice (coconut milk) straight from the fruit.

Back at General Luna, the laid-back island lifestyle revs up at night, as locals and visitors alike toast to another day of sweet surf and golden sunshine. At Triangle Siargao, you're five minutes from the main party strip, close enough to pop in at your leisure yet far enough away to hunker down in your A-frame in the tropics and enjoy the perfumed jungle breezes.

The Peak House,
page 194

3

Mountain

ALPENGLOW CABIN

This stunning cabin nestled in rugged Colorado mountain wilderness is a testament to the power of brilliant white paint and clean Scandinavian design. The 2019 reno of a two-decade-old, 1,226-square-foot (114 sq m) cabin turned a dark and downright dowdy home into a bright, light mountain aerie.

The transformation was a family affair, the work of two brothers, their spouses, and a couple of sons. They ripped up cork floors and old carpet and replaced them with beautiful wood plank flooring. A clunky pellet stove was swapped out for a soapstone HearthStone wood-burning stove. Pine cabinets in the kitchen were replaced with handmade open shelves of black walnut. Throughout the cabin, vintage touches (antique copper faucets, a farmhouse sink) are mixed with fashionable furnishings like sleek leather barstools and velvet armchairs. The result is a Scandi-rustic interior that's both cleanly modern and ultracomfy.

Alpenglow sits at the base of Independence Pass, looking up into the gorgeous mountainscape of La Plata Peak and (from the back) Mount Elbert—two of Colorado's "fourteeners" (mountains with peaks over 14,000 feet/4,267 m tall)—and is backed by national forestland.

Snow-tinged peaks and towering evergreens face the spacious wraparound deck, outfitted with wooden Muskoka chairs, a gas grill, and a hot tub for soaking with a view.

The setting also puts you close to some of Colorado's most celebrated outdoor activities, including backcountry skiing and snowshoeing. Twin Lakes (named for the two glacial lakes at the foot of La Plata and Mount Elbert) are just a ten-minute drive away, and are a recreational hub for boating and trout fishing; trailheads for mountain treks on the Colorado Trail lie at the lake's edge. A half hour's drive takes you to Leadville, a Victorian mining village. Family-favorite ski resort Ski Cooper is a forty-minute drive away, and ten minutes beyond that is the world-class ski terrain of Copper Mountain.

Handmade macramé wall hangings and textured pillows add to the cabin's vibe of cozy comfort.

OPPOSITE *The DIY family reno of Alpenglow included swapping out a clunky pellet stove for the sleek soapstone wood-burner pictured here.*

A canoe rests on the rock-strewn shoreline of Twin Lakes, Colorado's two largest glacial lakes and a ten-minute drive from the cabin.

HATCHER PASS LODGE

Palmer, Alaska

Stand in the shadows of rugged snow-clad peaks for a while, and you'll start to realize just how small you are. It's a humbling experience, particularly in the glacier-sculpted bowl of Hatcher Pass, where nine sturdy little red A-frames brace against the elements high up in Alaska's Talkeetna Mountains. In summer, the tundra is flecked with purple lupine and fireweed; in winter, huge drifts of snow blanket the pass. Night skies swirl with northern lights and the radiant twinkle of the Milky Way. The mind-blowing scenery just doesn't quit.

The Hatcher Pass A-frame lodge was built in the 1960s by a Bostonian named Hap Wurlitzer, who was drawn to the Alaskan frontier as a young man through Jack London's adventure stories. At the time, skiers were coming from Anchorage (about 60 miles/97 km away) and using an old rope tow from the abandoned Independence gold mine to get to the slopes. Wurlitzer homesteaded 10 acres (4 ha) of Hatcher Pass (back when you could do that sort of thing), and he and a couple of buddies built the big A-frame out of 32-foot (9.8 m) beams from Bird Creek. They started grooming trails for Nordic skiing and welcoming the passing mountain adventurers with food and drink. The little red cabins soon followed, lined up in a cinematic fashion against the cobalt-blue Alaska sky.

The cabins are basic but clean and heated, with tables for card games and windows that showcase skyscraping Talkeetna peaks. Some have vaulted ceilings with lofts; others are single-floor units. Each has a composting toilet but no shower or running water (the lodge provides every cabin with a large jug of water to use for washing up), but a sauna lies just down the path from the lodge. The camp can accommodate thirty people total—which makes it ideal for big groups or families.

Although founder Hap Wurlitzer passed away late in 2020, the lodge has no plans to lose its endearing rusticity. You can still sample a cold beer and a slice of razzleberry pie in the main lodge, and slip silently to your cabin on snowshoes on an inky Alaskan night.

EASTERN THREDBO CEDAR CABIN

The image of Australia as a year-round beach destination is shattered from June to October, when ski season arrives. Yes, Australia has a ski season—it's short but intense. Powder hounds flock to high-country resorts like Thredbo, in the Snowy Mountains, where you can blast down the longest vertical in the country, the High Noon ski run, on Australia's highest mountain, Mount Kosciuszko.

Situated on the banks of the Thredbo River, this handsome cedar cabin offers unobstructed views of both mountain and lift. Its spare, modern design is so striking that it was short-listed in a national design contest. Sydney designer Nicholas Gurney and owner and photographer Monique Easton collaborated on the remodel of the 1990s cedar cabin, with the goal of creating, as Easton puts it, "a study in Nordic minimalism." And they cut no corners: Natural and organic materials were used throughout; stained American oak ties the look together. Open-plan and loft-style, the space has vaulted ceilings with exposed beams, Scandi-cool bespoke furniture, even a private art collection. Objets include Scandinavian handheld lamps. Best of all, the cabin is glamping at its most comfortable and energy efficient. It even has a piping-hot Japanese-inspired glazed *onsen* for steamy soaking.

In winter, the icy setting in a forest of Australian silver gums is straight out of a Japanese lithograph. In summer, the burbling river next to the cabin becomes a swimming hole and fly-fishing playground. You can reach the top of Kosciuszko year-round by walking, mountain biking, or skiing, but you can also take a leisurely ride up on the Kosciuszko Express Chairlift for panoramic mountaintop viewing. Thredbo village, a two-minute walk from the cabin, has some thirty restaurants, bars, and bakeries. What could be better? You're in luck: A schnapps distillery, the Wildbrumby, is just a twenty-minute drive away. Grab a bottle or two for some bracing après-ski tippling.

The cabin's clean, minimalist form highlights its use of natural materials. Large windows let the outdoors shine.

Right by the cabin is the Thredbo River, which winds its way through the wintry landscape of Australia's Snowy Mountains.

BONNIE BELLE CABIN

The high country in Colorado's San Juan Mountains is the dominion of big mountains, big skies, and jaw-dropping vistas. At the Bonnie Belle Cabin, you are at the center of monumental alpine terrain—it's just you and 10 acres (4 ha) of snow-dappled granite peaks, rolling green tundra, and magnificent views.

This handsome log house makes for the perfect adventure base camp, hiking distance from craggy 14,000-foot-tall (4,267 m) mountains just begging to be climbed and fine fishing holes and wildflower meadows. The belle of the ball (sorry) when it comes to mountain sports and heli-skiing, the Bonnie Belle is an absolute bucket-list stay for anyone who appreciates the fierce beauty of the high country.

Bonnie Belle Cabin is 15 miles (24 km) north of Silverton, Colorado, in San Isabel National Forest. It's available to rent from June to late September and is accessible only by 4x4, ATV, foot, or dirt bike via off-road mountain trails. But this two-story cabin is no bare-bones backcountry hut. Solar powered and warmed by wood fire, the 1,200-square-foot (111 sq m) cabin is solidly built and comfortably upgraded, with a full kitchen, three bedrooms, and a sprawling living-room sectional below big picture windows. Rough-hewn beams line wood ceilings. A projector and 50-inch (127 cm) screen are on hand for movie night. Drop some cedar logs in the rugged black woodstove for instant ambience.

You're still talking off-grid mountain backcountry, though, so expect to rough it a little. The bathroom is an outhouse with a solar shower bag, located 50 feet (15 m) from the cabin; future upgrades include a thousand-gallon cistern and a gussied-up outhouse with a real shower. The house has no Wi-Fi or sat phones, and you'll have to bring in all your food and drink. So far, no one's complaining. Not with those surreal views and two redwood decks for sitting and sipping and taking it all in. As one guest said, "The deck on the Bonnie Belle even makes beer taste better."

Thanks to the area's pollution-free night skies, "you won't see stars like this anywhere else in the world," says co-owner Aaron Dodds.

FIRVALE WILDERNESS CAMP

This is not your grandmother's base camp. High up in remote mountain wilderness, just outside beautiful Tweedsmuir Provincial Park in the Bella Coola Valley, Firvale Wilderness Camp is nestled in the heart of the Great Bear Rainforest. The scenery is epic, a lyrical landscape of evergreen forest, glaciers, and waterfalls—and grizzlies! It's also one of the world's great outdoor playgrounds. Here you can hike mountain trails, raft glacial rivers, heli-ski backcountry drifts, soak in remote hot springs, and fish salmon-rich waters. But in between all that fevered adventuring, the owners of Firvale believe you deserve some cocooning comfort, and their collection of A-frame cabins and geodesic glamping domes brings base camp into the twenty-first century.

The cabins come with en suite bathrooms (with showers), patios, and cozy lofts. Eco-friendly amenities include recycled wool throws and organic bath products. A step up on the glamping ladder, the geodesic domes are spacious and stylish. The handsome post-and-beam cookhouse is the camp's communal kitchen

and lounge, with leather couches, oversize windows, and tables for dining. The wood-fired Firvale sauna, in a separate building, was crafted from locally sourced wood and is a soothing finish to an active day.

The Monarch Icefield, visible from each cabin, is the second largest ice cap in British Columbia; Firvale can arrange a heli hike on the glacier. The Bella Coola Valley is also home to the highest free-falling waterfall in Canada, Hunlen Falls—hike the 10 miles (16 km) to the falls or see it by floatplane leaving from Nimpo Lake.

Anglers flock to the Bella Coola and Atnarko Rivers to fish for salmon and trout—and you might not be the only one out trolling for a big one. The Bella Coola Valley is prime grizzly terrain, especially from September to October, when the river salmon run. Firvale provides hikers with bear bells and spray, and bear platforms offer convenient lookout locations. For an even closer look, book a river raft trip led by indigenous Nuxalk guides, and marvel as you slowly glide by grizzly families while they hunt for salmon at the icy water's edge.

The interior of a Firvale dome, with a king-size bed, sheepskin-clad chairs, and showstopping views.

LEFT *Jumbo outdoor soaker tubs come complete with essential-oil bath salts.*

BELOW *The A-frames were crafted from second-growth cedar harvested from the Bella Coola Valley.*

Firvale is bear country, and one of the best places to spot one is on a guided river rafting trip.

OPPOSITE Guests dine on chunky log stools in the communal post-and-beam cookhouse.

Every cabin and dome in the 13-acre (5.3 ha) camp shares the same unbelievable views of glacial ice fields and snow-glazed mountains.

RED MOUNTAIN ALPINE LODGE

This beautiful custom-built timber-frame lodge in the heart of Colorado's San Juan Mountains brings European-style mountain hutting to the US. As one fan put it, it's backcountry but better. Here comfort, style, and premium food and drink are as essential to the alpine experience as the matchless wilderness adventures right outside the lodge's big iron door.

High up where the mountains meet the sky, the Red Mountain Alpine Lodge hovers in the clouds at an elevation of 11,000 feet (3,353 m). It's just off Highway 550 but right at Red Mountain Pass, home to the russet-tinged trio of alpine peaks known as the Red Mountains—the heart of Colorado backcountry skiing. This unbeatable location gives you out-the-door access to premier wilderness and 14,000-foot (4,267 m) slopes packed with deep, pristine powder. Expect snow and lots of it: Red Mountain Pass gets some 300 inches (7.6 m) annually.

The lodge sleeps up to twenty-two people, with three private bedrooms on the first floor and a second-floor loft with ten beds. Renting out the entire lodge is popular with groups and families for gatherings and retreats. When it comes to wining and dining, this place means business: There's a marble kitchen island, a wine cellar, a coffee bar, and a tavern for hot toddies and craft beer. Breakfast and dinner (plus snacks and afternoon tea) are included and prepared fresh by a chef daily, and a long farm table is set for communal meals. The lodge is solar powered, with radiant in-floor heating and Wi-Fi but no cell-phone service.

Come to ski or snowshoe in winter and hike San Juan forest trails in summer. The San Juans hold about 5 million acres (2 million ha) of protected wilderness and national forestland and more than six hundred mountains—an all-season playground for adventure seekers. The Red Mountain Alpine Lodge owners also run San Juan Mountain Guides in nearby Ouray, providing local guides for ski expeditions, ice and rock climbs, and treks that conveniently leave from the lodge's front door.

The lodge is 3,000 square feet (279 sq m) of rugged Douglas fir and exposed post-and-beam timber. The look is elevated alpine-rustic; the ambience cozy après-ski.

HINTERHOUSE

Less is definitely more in this stunning cabin in the rugged forests of the Laurentian Mountains. There's nothing extraneous or obtrusive here—it's the minimal, earthy opposite of baroque adornment. Solid, sustainable, natural materials become connective threads to the outside: The house is clad in native white cedar, ceilings are oiled planks of red pine, floors are poured and heated concrete, and ebony-stained Douglas fir forms the kitchen back wall. What's striking about all this restraint is the cabin's meditative comfort and livability. You really want to hang your hat here.

Designed by architect David Dworkind of the Ménard Dworkind studio, Hinterhouse is a 930-square-foot (86 sq m) shoebox of a cabin that manages to feel spacious thanks to thoughtful design touches: Sliding shutters designed to echo the cedar cladding can be opened up for full immersion in the outdoors or shut for complete privacy. The Hinterhouse is drenched in sunlight from floor-to-ceiling windows—60 percent of the cabin is clad in glass (including a wall of the shower!). In the center of the open-plan living area, a wood-burning stove rotates 360 degrees. A farmhouse table made of maple doubles as a kitchen island with a built-in vessel sink. Sliding panels in bedrooms hide TVs.

Hinterhouse is nestled into slopes of dense boreal forest with panoramic views of the Mont-Tremblant valley. A staircase carved into the hillside leads to a four-person sauna cabin and an outdoor shower. The 600-acre (243 ha) Mont-Tremblant Ski Resort, just a fifteen-minute drive away, offers first-rate skiing, fat-tire biking, snowshoeing, and dogsledding, as well as a pedestrian village of shops and cafés; in summer, visitors head to Lake Tremblant for fishing, water-skiing, and even swimming—the mountain lake warms up to a balmy 68°F (20°C).

Hinterhouse is the first in what the Hinter company hopes will be a long line of prefab cabins. To give back, the company has pledged to plant ten trees for every booking. It's a refreshing paradigm—a seamless integration of art, nature, and true sustainability. We could all soon be living in a happy world of Hinterhouses. Sign us up!

The focal point of the living/dining area is a black wood-burning stove that rotates 360 degrees.

OPPOSITE The spare, white-tiled bathroom has concrete floors and a shower with a floor-to-ceiling window.

Sliding shutters designed to echo the cedar siding can be opened up to bring the outdoors in or closed for complete privacy.

ALPINE LAKES HIGH CAMP

The Pacific Northwest doesn't lack for cozy cabination, but these nine rustic huts in Washington State's Cascade Range offer access to pristine backcountry few ever get to see. Perched at an altitude of 5,000 feet (1,524 m), way up in the rugged peaks and folds of the Alpine Lakes Wilderness, the High Camp is set inside a wonderland of massive firs and snow-dusted mountains, mirrored in shimmering lakes.

The High Camp is a year-round destination, offering warm-weather mountain biking and hikes through huckleberry patches and wildflower meadows. The camp has an inflatable stand-up paddleboard, and fat mountain trout make for great fishing. But winter is when these cabins shine, with access to off-trail slopes for high-country skiing and telemarking (free-heel alpine skiing). You'll be plowing through pristine powder under blue skies and gunmetal peaks. Snowboarding, snowshoeing, and fat-tire biking promise high-thrills explorations.

Après-whatever, your nights are spent in simple but sturdy A-frame wood huts. There's nothing fancy about these cabins, but all are cozy and built to last. Two sit near the creek that tumbles through camp; others are a stone's throw from the main trails. All are equipped with the backcountry basics: propane cooking stove and lamps, cookware, platforms with mattresses and pillows, and table and chairs. Woodstoves keep things toasty when the temperature drops, while decks offer unobstructed Pacific Northwest views.

How do you get to all this blissful backcountry? Simply park your ride in a guest parking lot some 8 miles (13 km) below. You are then convoyed to High Camp via SUVs tricked out with snow tracks. You can end your trip the same way or with a leisurely ski down to the lot where you parked your car in what feels like another lifetime. The long, hushed ski down gives you plenty of time to contemplate your sojourn in the rarefied air above.

ECOCAMP PATAGONIA

The work of a dynamic planet is frozen in the multihued layers of rock at the Torres del Paine National Park in Chile's Patagonia. It tells the story of hot magma and glacial ice, and the folding and faulting of the earth's crust to build mountains. The jagged triplet towers (the Torres del Paine) rise some 5,000 feet (1,524 m) above a turquoise lake in a brazen show of sheer verticality.

When you stay at EcoCamp, your backyard is that park and those peaks; the wild, stark beauty of Patagonia surrounds you. This dynamic terrain enfolds mountains, deciduous forest, grassy plains, and Andean desert. Operated by Chilean tour operator Cascada Expediciones, this sustainable geodesic-dome "hotel" complex makes a spectacular base camp for a multitude of Patagonian adventures, from glacier ice treks to hiking the "W," the 31-mile (50 km) route that takes you past such jaw-dropping sights as Grey Glacier and the Torres themselves. You can kayak icy rivers or mountain bike grassy valleys. Wild-horse safaris go in search of the rare Patagonian horses whose lineage dates back to the Spanish conquistadors. You can track other wildlife, too, including the camel-like guanaco and the elusive puma, known as the "ghost cat" of the region thanks to its silky stealth.

Hydro and solar power provide 95 percent of the energy used at the camp. You partake of locally sourced foods (and wines) in large community domes, warmed by woodstoves and pelt-strewn chairs. The living domes range from basic with shared bathrooms and no heating or electricity to whopping two-floor heated domes with low-emission woodstoves, private terraces, and private bathrooms with state-of-the-art composting toilets.

You can watch the starry night skies from your bed through skylights, which serve double duty by capturing the sun's heat during the day. Getting a leg up on the weather in Patagonia is key: As it's been famously noted, you can experience four seasons in a single day here, and the changes come fast. The wind can be fierce, with some of the strongest westerlies in the world. But you'll be cozy inside your eco dome—all come with padded walls and thick fleece blankets.

All domes come with padded walls and thick fleece blankets for warmth, and skylights for stargazing. Superior Domes, like this one, also have private bathrooms.

OPPOSITE *EcoCamp domes follow the "leave no trace" footprints of the dwellings of Patagonia's ancient nomadic tribes: infrastructure that's easy to build in and pack out with minimal damage to the land.*

Purple lupine and ice-tipped mountains frame the EcoCamp Welcome Dome.

LAGÖM

A glass box inside a wood temple, this cabin is a stone-cold stunner. Just a thirty-minute drive from Quebec City, the secluded Lagöm cabin overlooks the vast emerald forests of the Laurentian Mountains and the curves of the Saint Lawrence River. It sits up above the tree line at a fresh-air altitude of 1,969 feet (600 m) atop Mont Tourbillon. It's a magnificent spot, one that gives you direct access to the extensive trail system of Sentiers du Moulin, an outdoor recreation area famed for world-class mountain biking and skiing, snowboarding, and snowshoeing through backcountry terrain.

Three sides of glass walls showcase all that cinematic scenery, expanding the 376 square feet (35 sq m) of living space. A tiered deck leads right to the edge of the forest abyss—sheer drama. Lagöm is solar powered and gas heated, and everything inside has a pared-down polish: wood and glass, glass and wood, with the occasional Scandi-cozy punctuation point like textured furry pillows, a fringed slate blanket, hanging basket lamps. The neutral palette inside is a serene contrast

to the spectacle outdoors. The *salle de bain* is a masterwork of compact scale, with a stylish rain-shower head. The sofa downstairs becomes a comfy bed; a king bed in the mezzanine has stunning mountain views. An outdoor firepit has a stovepipe shapeliness, and it pumps out the heat.

At Sentiers du Moulin, mountain bikers take to the challenging singletracks—forest trails that snake, switchback, and drop over rock, dirt, and pallet-plank bridges. In winter, riders with beefy fat tires hit the 12 miles (19 km) of snowy trails for a cold-weather "Enduro" version of the super G mountain-bike trail. Le Relais ski center, the century-old pioneer of Quebec City skiing, has downhill and cross-country skiing and snowboarding parks—it even offers a *ski acrobatique* school for those with a jones for freestyle jumping. Swimming and boat rentals are available at Club Nautique, and Lac-Beauport Outfitters can arrange fishing, horseback-riding and dogsledding expeditions. The cabin is a ten-minute drive from the town of Lac-Beauport, but the off-grid seclusion here makes it feel light-years away.

DUNTON HOT SPRINGS

Dolores, Colorado

Back in the 1880s, the Colorado gold-rush settlement of Dunton was home to a scrappy cast of characters, from miners and homesteaders to outlaws and hucksters. Perched in an alpine valley in the Colorado Rockies (8,600-foot/2,621 m elevation), Dunton was built around a huddle of hand-hewn log cabins, a saloon, and hot mineral springs. When the railroad arrived in Colorado, the town's three hundred or so residents up and left to be closer to the train tracks. The last inhabitant abandoned Dunton in 1918. In the ensuing years, the ghost town took on a range of rakish identities: It was a hippie hangout in the 1970s and a bikers' camp in the '80s. It wasn't until the early twenty-first century that the dilapidated old miners' town found resurrection as an haute version of itself, with much of its frontier character wonderfully intact.

Today every cabin on-site is authentic and hand-built (although a few were brought in from other towns in Colorado). The oldest, Bjoerkmans cabin, was constructed by a Scandinavian settler sometime in the 1880s. All told, the 500-acre (202 ha) resort can accommodate up

to forty-four guests. In spite of the fact that the cabins are outfitted with luxe modern comforts like radiant-floor heating, the resort maintains a palpable Old West feel. Charcoal graffiti from the turn of the twentieth century graces the walls of the old Bathhouse. Guests dine at long tables in the saloon. In 1889, Robert LeRoy Parker, aka Butch Cassidy, had a drink at the bar after robbing a bank in nearby Telluride. It was his first bank heist, and the cheeky outlaw carved his name into the bar top. True or not, it's a good story—and BUTCH remains etched in the wood.

The resort offers high-mountain horseback riding, fly-fishing on the Dolores River, hiking and mountain biking, and rock climbing. In winter, you can explore the San Juan peaks by snowshoe or cross-country ski on trails laid out by a former Olympic Nordic skier. Dunton's geothermal hot springs are still percolating, and they're not the only geothermal waters around; sample them all on the Colorado Historic Hot Springs Loop, a 720-mile (1,159 km) driving tour of some seventeen hot-springs experiences.

MOUNTAIN 183

Guests can soak in geothermal hot springs inside the nineteenth-century Bathhouse.

OPPOSITE *The two-level Dunton Springs library has a wide selection of books, a roaring fireplace, and sippin' whiskey for guests.*

When the twilight snow is piled
this deep, the time is ripe for
snowshoeing, skiing (and heli-skiing),
snowmobiling, and sleigh rides.

JOFFRE CREEK CABINS

Pemberton,
British Columbia,
Canada

At Joffre Creek Cabins, a rapturous setting of unsullied mountain forest and ice-blue lakes meets two heavenly log cabins (and a vintage Airstream) for pure British Columbia bliss. Ringed by park wilderness, the secluded 3.5-acre (1.4 ha) complex is the closest lodging to the three spectacular glacial lakes of Joffre Lakes Provincial Park, which spill down the mountains into the falls of Lower Joffre Creek. This is the (BC) life: Kick back on the front deck, snug in the warmth of a propane firepit, with the jagged, snow-tipped peaks of a mountain glacier framed in firs before you.

The Big Cabin is 2,000 square feet (186 sq m) of comfy curated space. The great room is a brawny ode to wood and leather, with an antique woodstove loaded and ready to fire up when you arrive. A six-person hot tub gets you out in the alpine air. The Little Cabin (pictured opposite) is 800 square feet (74 sq m) of chunky log cabin with a screened-in gazebo lined in fairy lights. Lower on the property, a restored 1970 Airstream Overlander has a cedar gazebo that lights up expeditiously at happy hour. It's just one of many cool little touches in the complex, along with dog biscuits for your puppies and fresh shower loofahs. The seclusion here is the real deal: The only neighbors around are grizzlies, black bears, foxes, coyotes, and moose.

In prime hiking season (June to September), a path to the three lakes (Lower, Middle, and Upper Joffre) meanders through green valleys; forests of towering hemlock, fir, and spruce; and open fields of boulders scattered by glaciers on the move. Listen for the bone-rattling crack of ice sheering off the Matier Glacier. In winter, when the lakes freeze over, you can still hike the snowy terrain; just bring your snowshoes or wear shoes with spikes or crampons.

The cabins are a big draw for serious skiers, too; you're forty minutes by car to the knee-deep powder at legendary Whistler Blackcomb. You're even closer to a drive up Duffey Lake Road, one of BC's most scenic routes. It's 62 miles (100 km) of curvy switchback roads from nearby Pemberton to Lillooet. But it's worth it for the gorgeous BC mountain scenery and the chance to spot black bears, mule deer, and mountain goats along the way.

RIGHT *The property's vintage Airstream has its own cedar shower shack, with a big clawfoot tub for long, hot soaks.*

BELOW *The Big Cabin has an original Eames chair and ottoman draped in a Hudson Bay blanket.*

OPPOSITE *The Little Cabin's sun-filled living area has a loft ladder to the bedroom above.*

Strings of fairy lights come on automatically at dusk above the Airstream.

OPPOSITE *A hammock hangs in a stand of forest pines, with glimpses of mountain glaciers through the trees.*

THE PEAK HOUSE

The Slovenian Alps look like something out of a fairy tale. Cows graze hillside pastures, and waterfalls spill into emerald pools. Medieval villages and shepherd's huts are tucked into valleys of green. At the turn of the twentieth century, the Slovenian Alps became a draw for mountaineers after local climbers developed a well-marked system of trails. Over the years, some 180 wilderness huts, cabins, and bivouacs (temporary shelters) have been built along the more than 6,200 miles (10,000 km) of trails for backcountry climbers to use as outposts from the often harsh conditions (camping in the wild is prohibited). Many are lodges offering rib-sticking comfort food (venison goulash, stews, and strudel). Others are basic bivouacs with little to no facilities (let alone provisions), just refuge from the bitter winter cold.

In 2015, a rusted fifty-year-old hut in a treacherous, remote setting—on the craggy plateau atop Mount Skuta overlooking the Skuta glacier—was in need of replacement. (Mount Skuta, at 8,307 feet/2,532 m high, is the country's third-largest peak, an old soul of stone and ice.) The hut received a high-concept makeover,

in a remarkable international collaboration between Harvard University students, Slovenian architects, and British engineers. The new shelter, called Peak House, is composed of three modules that were prefabricated off-site, then flown by helicopter to the ridge.

Inspired by the country's traditional alpine architecture, the Peak House is designed to provide maximum protection against extreme weather conditions and avalanches. An exterior of reinforced concrete cladding not only serves as insulation but also blends in aesthetically with the gray mountain hues. Triple-glazed structural glass offers both protection and unobstructed viewing of the surrounding mountain peaks. An interior of honeyed wood holds bunks for up to eight people and spaces for food prep, storage, and socializing. Benches double as tables and fold-down beds. The tiered peaks mirror the mountains around them. The house's designers succeeded in creating a durable structure that's also compact and easy to assemble and remove. Most important, it provides sturdy shelter for any mountaineer who reaches these glorious heights.

A wall of glass allows guests to look out over the Skuta Glacier from high atop Mount Skuta.

THE TREEHOUSE UTAH

Park City, Utah

The tree is *in* the house at Treehouse Utah. For real. We're talking a knobby, gnarled, two-hundred-year-old, much-loved Utah alpine fir that propels its massive trunk up through two levels of house and is as much a member of the main-bedroom milieu as its occupants.

Given the remoteness of this rural community and a local no-hunting policy, the area is a refuge for all types of wildlife. The resident bull moose, nicknamed Marvin the Moose by the cheeky owners, Gianni and Rocky Donati, routinely wanders through the property. "He believes that the watering tank at the end of our driveway is his personal drinking hole," says Rocky. Other beloved neighbors are a family of owls named Ozzy, Merlin, and Gandalf (yes, the couple names everything).

Treehouse Utah welcomes human visitors as well, and apparently people love it as much as the wildlife does. And what's not to love? The treehouse has been beautifully upgraded, transformed from a primitive cabin on stilts into not only a modern home with running water, electricity, and a heating system but also a superstylish mountain-canyon retreat. The kitchen is small, with a mini fridge/freezer and a single induction stovetop, but it has all the tools you need for cooking. A cedar deck looks out onto Utah's magnificent Uinta Mountains. Big windows throughout are like a speed date with nature. The luxe lofted bedroom has a skylight for stargazing, and the shower is a dreamy mosaic of multicolored stone. Oh, and the house *has a tree growing through it.*

Rocky and Gianni live in their "chalet" next door, and a rural canyon community is located up a rugged access road—you'll need a 4x4/AWD vehicle to traverse the last 3 miles (4.8 km) of dirt. When you get there, you'll be up in the clouds, at an elevation of 8,000 feet (2,438 m). Yet you're still less than a twenty-minute drive to Park City, Utah's world-class recreational playground, offering some of the finest ski resorts in the world, summertime river rafting and tubing down the Weber and Provo Rivers, and scenic drives through gorgeous mountain passes.

198   CABIN TRIPPING

An annual health check with an arborist helps owners Rocky and Gianni Donati keep tabs on their "little baby." Fortunately, trees are pretty self-sustaining, and upkeep is little more than routine branch pruning and sap watching (sap production is a telltale sign of health).

OPPOSITE This rural canyon community is a refuge for all types of wildlife, including a bull moose named Marvin, who routinely ambles around the property. The big treehouse windows ensure you don't miss a sighting.

LA CABIN
RIDE & SLEEP

This handsome little cabin has a big setting, perched on a ledge of the highest mountain in the Laurentians, Mont Tourbillon, and looking out over evergreen forests and broad-shouldered peaks. The 11-acre (4.5 ha) property is secluded and sublime, but if you're a mountain biker (like the cabin's owner), the location is even sweeter. The outdoor recreation area of Sentiers du Moulin, at the foot of the mountain, draws bikers from all over the world for its daredevil singletrack trails and 12 miles (19 km) of fat-tire winter tracks. With trails practically right out the door, La Cabin was literally built for guests who want to ride and sleep.

La Cabin is compact—430 square feet (40 sq m)—but feels roomy, thanks to 20-foot (6 m) ceilings, sliding glass doors, and wide windows that take in the outdoors. This off-grid eco-cabin is solar powered and warmed by a propane heater and woodstove. It has neither AC nor TV, but it's built for glamping comfort. The aesthetic is minimalist, a testament to Scandi-style simplicity and the reliable solidity of wood: Cedar, larch, and aspen line the interior, and the kitchen features chunky handmade

log stools and cabinets adorned with *shou sugi ban*, the ancient Japanese technique of preserving wood through fire. The upstairs bedrooms—an en suite and a kids' bunk room—are reached via a wood ladder.

Outside is a patio for soaking up that monumental mountain panorama, plus a firepit and a picnic table. A covered porch on the A-frame's back side has a hammock, and there's even an outdoor shower for a post–bike ride rinse. Watching the sun melt over the mountains from the deck, firepit blazing, is nirvana in any season.

The privacy of the cabin is absolute, but civilization (groceries, restaurants, stuff) is just a ten-minute drive away. You're close to ski resorts offering downhill and cross-country and snowboarding and lakes for boating and swimming. In winter, bring snowshoes (*raquettes*) to explore the snowy forest terrain. The town of Lac-Beauport has all you need for your cabin adventure—plus Nordic spas and a "sugar shack" museum/shop offering traditional sugar-bush meals, music, and maple sugar goodies.

The views from the glassed-in living area include spectacular sunsets over the Laurentians.

OPPOSITE The hammock on La Cabin's back porch makes an ideal perch for summertime reverie.

La Cabin's secluded setting in the evergreen forests of the Laurentian Mountains is close to singletrack mountain-bike trails and fat-tire trails for winter biking.

HIGH COUNTRY CABIN

Ben Ohau,
Pukaki Ward,
New Zealand

Hunker down and unplug in the alps—the Southern Alps, that is—at this bucolic wilderness cabin rimmed by silvery peaks and green pastures of grazing sheep. Home to New Zealand's highest mountains, the Southern Alps form the backbone of the country's South Island. This is where Northern Hemisphereans sweating out summer's heat go for a real Kiwi winter adventure, as snowfields and ski resorts and glaciers are all within easy reach.

It's the perfect place to practice the arts of alpinism (climbing mountains) and tramping (hiking mountain trails). The area is also a hot spot for world-class fly-fishing in South Island rivers and streams. Nearby is New Zealand's longest glacier, the Tasman, which you can see by boat or kayak, on foot, or by 4WD. You can even ski on it, a bucket-list must-do if ever there was one. Or you can stay put in the cabin, sip hot cocoa, indulge in a few fireplace selfies, and swear to anyone who asks that you did all of the above.

Cradled in alpine desert grasslands, midway between Christchurch and Queenstown (and close enough to the adorably named town of Twizel to run for goods and grub when you need it), the 538-square-foot (50 sq m) cabin is stylishly customized, warmed by sunlight streaming through picture windows as big as Texas and a cozy log burner fed by kindling you chop yourself. The comfy furnishings trend Western rustic, from antler chandeliers to cowhide rugs. Hanging pots and pans and polished wood cabinets give the little kitchen a homey chuck-wagon appeal.

Best of all, you'll have the cabin and surrounding 10 acres (4 ha) all to yourself, and the views of the Ben Ohau Range go on forever: waving grasses in summer, icy rock and scrub in winter, and always, always sheep—sometimes grazing and gazing right at you. Get away from it all, chop some wood, tramp a glacier, or just soak in all that Southern Alps scenery.

OPPOSITE *The homey kitchen has concrete floors and raw-edged wood counters.*

LEFT *The steel-roofed cabin sits on 10 acres (4 ha) of alpine desert grasslands surrounded by icy, rugged peaks.*

BELOW *These grasslands are home to herds of sheep, which don't mind peeking into cabin windows during grazing hours.*

A stay in New Zealand's Southern Alps is a chance to take scenic flights and make glacier landings in Mount Cook National Park.

The cabin's wild, isolated setting was the site of the Battle of the Pelennor Fields, a key sequence in the third Lord of the Rings film.

MAISON TETONIA

Maison Tetonia is a John Ford Western come to life. With a hitching post out front and snow-crested peaks out back, this little wood cabin in the Tetons was reputedly the creation of a set designer enamored of the lore of the American West—and he nailed it. The wooden porch is a cowboy mélange of whiskey barrels and wagon wheels, crowned with a SALOON sign. The Old West theme doesn't stop at the door; inside, unvarnished walls of knotty pine are hung with weathered saddles and horseshoes.

Maison Tetonia pays homage to a simpler time, but it doesn't stint on modern conveniences—it has heating, Wi-Fi, hot water, a full kitchen, even a washer-dryer. A gas fireplace offsets the chill when temperatures drop at nightfall. The open-concept living area is replete with leather couches and colorful throws, but the star attraction is the pool table perched on a cowhide rug. In the bedroom is a big iron bed and a sweet miniature braided rug on the night table, plus other vintage tchotchkes. Outside, there's a saltwater hot tub (with a wagon-hut changing room!) and a firepit; linger a while and you might spot a meteor shower or shooting star.

This 10-acre (4 ha) property is ringed by blue skies and Tetons peaks. It's crazy quiet here, the hush broken only by the rustling of sagebrush and the rippling of a rock-strewn creek (fine for toe-dipping on hot summer days). Three black stallions in the pasture next door are ridiculously photogenic, just one more in a long queue of stunning Instagrammable moments out on the prairie.

You can hike aspen trails just a fifteen-minute drive from the cabin or take the ninety-minute drive to Grand Teton National Park, which has more than 210 miles (338 km) of hiking trails that traverse backcountry grassland and rugged peaks. The cabin is also ninety minutes from Yellowstone by car. The world-class skiing and snowboarding nearby include the tony runs at Jackson Hole Mountain Resort, an hour's drive away. You can fish for trout in summer and winter (ice fishing) in rivers and lakes, and take a languid cruise down the Teton River in just about anything that floats—including inner tubes.

THE NOOQ

When a mountain is your backyard, it makes sense to go big. The Nooq cabin is all about big spaces: cathedral ceilings, fat soaking tubs, and enormous glass windows. It's also about big ideas: the clean elegance of Scandinavian design, the luminous warmth of natural light. The Nooq gets it all right, ticking off a perfect balance of style, comfort, and killer setting. Since it was completed in 2019, this contemporary retreat in Whitefish, Montana, has become a style icon. Everyone, it seems, wants to live in a Nooq.

The custom work of two globetrotting photographers, Andrea Dabene and Alex Strohl, this 2,600-square-foot (242 sq m) home is tucked into a hillside forest of conifers and wildflowers but is close enough to the slopes of nearby Whitefish Mountain Resort to have ski-in access. The Nooq is roomy, with three bedrooms and three and a half baths. In the spacious living area, an entire wall of gabled windows overlooks a forest of firs and pines. The sculptural centerpiece of the room is the floating Fireorb hearth. Just off the main room, an expansive deck with lounge seating and a firepit hovers over a vast forest gorge that spills down to the valley below.

But the most stunning design feature just may be the handcrafted glass tile from the California company Fireclay Tile. Each bathroom's shower has its own gorgeous hue: one the color of mountain lakes, another the yellow-orange tinge of fall leaves. The kitchen backsplash, in a Fireclay flagstone, is set against a black quartz countertop and wood cabinets. The Nooq is full of other just-so design touches, too, like dried flowers in clear tube sconces above a bed, and sliding doors that open and close with pull handles made for chests of drawers.

Whitefish lies on the fringes of Glacier National Park, where you can hike, bike, fish, ice climb, and ski. Locals have been skiing Whitefish's own "Big Mountain" since 1947. The chill local vibe is still a hallmark of the Whitefish ski resort, where the lines are famously short and snow is practically guaranteed: The area averages some 300 inches (7.6 m) of snow a year. Watching it fall from the other side of that wall of glass, Fireorb simmering, is hygge on high.

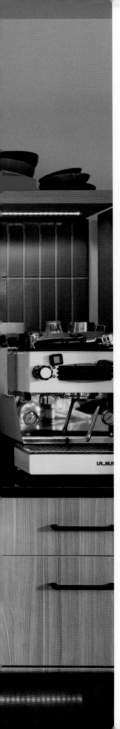

A patterned wool rug from Oaxaca pops against a sea of neutrals in the dining area.

OPPOSITE *The Fireclay flagstone tile is a colorful contrast to the kitchen's black quartz countertop and blond wood cabinetry.*

A tub with a view: In the master bathroom, take a soak in the freestanding curved tub from Wetstyle.

OPPOSITE *Wintry evenings like this one are common at the Nooq—the Whitefish region averages more than 300 inches (8 m) of snow annually.*

IDYLLCREEK A-FRAME

Idyllwild,
California

The mile-high village of Idyllwild lies in the ponderosa pines of the San Jacinto Mountains. This small town has a larger-than-life past: In the 1800s, the gold rush came to town, but prospectors left empty-handed. Lumber mills and cattle ranches followed, after which Hollywood came calling, and filmmakers like Cecil B. DeMille made movies here. Writer Timothy Leary lived on a ranch in the mountain foothills, cooking up LSD with a band of hippie surfers. But the mountain wilderness also attracted rock climbers, bluegrass musicians, artists, and recreational campers. Catering to visitors became the main business of "Idyllwild in the Pines."

Idyllwild's budding tourism industry happily coincided with a national movement toward wilderness preservation, and in 1937, the Mount San Jacinto State Park was dedicated. Today Idyllwild and its boho mountain culture are attracting new generations of outdoor lovers, who flock to legendary rock formations Tahquitz and Suicide Rocks and fish for rainbow trout in nearby Lake Hemet.

Experience Idyllwild, a family-owned business offering vacation rental, runs six Idyllwild cabins of varying vintages, each a cozy throwback to American rusticity. Idyllcreek A-Frame, surrounded by tall pines, is a standout of the bunch. The wood-burning fireplace and outdoor hot tub pretty much seal the deal, but the cottage is so much more. Wide steps lead up to a good-size patio with a table and chairs, a hot tub, and a firepit. A tree grows right through the deck. Sunlight floods the cabin's living area thanks to floor-to-ceiling windows, and buttery leather sofas are made for curling up in front of the big woodstove. The river-rock shower in the downstairs bathroom was hand-built by the owner. A spiral staircase leads to a loft with high peaked beams and a king bed with a colorful Pendleton spread. The kitchen is compact but fully stocked for most any kind of cooking.

If you feel like fishing for trout but don't want to travel far, drop a line in Strawberry Creek, which bubbles along not far from the cabin. The creek was named for the strawberries that still grow wild along the banks, living testament to Idyllwild's freewheeling soul.

Sheldon Mountain House,
page 236

Arctic

HATTVIKA LODGE

Since ancient times, fishermen have traveled by the thousands to the little Norwegian fishing villages of the Lofoten Islands for the late-winter spawning of the arctic cod (*lofotfiske*). In the nineteenth century, seasonal fishermen's huts known as *rorbuer* were constructed around the water's edge for shelter during winter lofotfiske runs. The traditional *rorbu* was a simple, single-story log hut often built out over the water on stilts. One room was for fishing equipment; the other was a basic kitchen/bunk room warmed by a wood-burning stove and lit by cod-liver-oil lamps—housing two men per (very short) bunk. It was all about the fish; creature comforts were secondary.

The cod of the ancient Lofoten fishery still make their northern migration, but these days the character-filled villages are welcoming another kind of migration: tourists drawn to the islands' remote and icy beauty. Throughout the Lofotens, rorbuer are getting stylish revamps for tourist stays, and historic buildings are being repurposed as galleries and cafés. At the Hattvika Lodge, in Ballstad, sixteen original rorbuer of various vintages have been beautifully restored and renovated with the kind of stylish comfort that few nineteenth-century fishermen ever experienced. In addition to its revitalized rorbuer, Hattvika Lodge has also built ten new hillside cabins that blend seamlessly into the quaint milieu. Inside, open-concept main rooms offer a real luxury of space and any modern conveniences you require, and the style is smart, pared-down Scandinavian. Bathrooms come with heated tile floors, and the beds are heaven to sink into.

Because of its central location in the Lofotens, Ballstad makes a fine base camp for any number of adventure activities, from sea kayaking (with flocks of sea eagles overhead) to ski mountaineering, hiking the nearby hills, and, yes, fishing—whether you rent your own boat, take a charter into the deep, or try a little arctic spearfishing under the midnight sun. You'll be just one more in a long line of visitors chasing the arctic cod in these northern seas.

*The fishermen's huts known
as rorbuer were often built
out over the rocky shoreline,
the easier to unload boats
full of freshly caught cod.*

Norway's Lofoten Islands are some of the best places on earth to see the northern lights.

PANORAMA GLASS LODGE

Among Iceland's infinite charms is watching the aurora borealis paint the northern skies in swirls of neon hues. The northern lights season in Iceland lasts a good seven months, from late August to April, and all you need is a clear, cloudless evening and a night sky peppered with stars. Some resorts offer an aurora borealis wake-up call in case you fall asleep waiting for the magic to happen. In the glass cabin igloos of the Panorama Glass Lodge, the skies do the waking.

A Reykjavík couple designed the original Panorama Glass Lodge as a romantic "bed with a view"—a house of steel and wood wrapped in triple glass on three sides (plus the ceiling) to allow visitors to soak in the scenic surrounds. The concept proved so popular that four glass cabins have been built near the town of Hella, along Iceland's southern coastline, home to thunderous waterfalls and sprawling glaciers. Heated by Iceland's geothermal springs, each house offers supercomfy beds with fine linens, a private bathroom, and unparalleled views that change dramatically with the seasons. A small kitchen offers full cooking and dinnerware supplies plus basic foodstuffs—you'll have to bring in any fresh foods and beverages. Enjoy that most Scandinavian of activities with a steaming soak in your outdoor hot tub under the stars. Handwoven hammocks and adult-size "Viking" swings make for breezy summertime relaxing.

The glass lodges are about a two-hour drive from the Reykjavík airport. A rental car will come in handy, as you'll want to take in the mind-blowing scenery of the Ring Road, Iceland's main highway. Halfway to Hella is the Golden Circle, an iconic loop road featuring one killer attraction after another, from steaming geysers to massive waterfalls to the lava fields of the Hekla volcano. Each cabin has its own ultraprivate setting, but all come with curtains. The hosts don't recommend them, however. From northern lights to icy peaks and shimmering tundra, you won't want to miss a thing.

The bathroom is full of stylish touches, including pendant lamps and a rock sink.

OPPOSITE *The open-plan glass cabin is roomy enough for a custom-made king bed, a kitchen, and a dining area.*

The snow-covered stratovolcano Hekla rises over the tundra surrounding the glass lodges.

SHELDON MOUNTAIN HOUSE

When it comes to adventuring, few figures in the history of the Alaska Range were more scrappy, skilled, or downright heroic than ace bush pilot Don Sheldon. Sheldon pioneered the technique of landing on glaciers in the 1950s, flying his little Piper Super Cub with retractable skis, to help map the Denali region; deliver supplies, equipment, and people to some of Alaska's most remote corners; and make countless rescues.

Over several flights in 1966, Sheldon brought lumber (strapped to the outside of the Super Cub) to a granite-and-ice outcrop overlooking Ruth Glacier to build his own backcountry cabin and a shelter for climbers, photographers, and skiers passing through. That sturdy little hexagonal hut is now available for rent from March through July.

To get to the cabin, you'll take a ski-plane from Talkeetna to a nearby airfield of packed-down snow. Then it's a fifteen-minute (0.3 mile/0.5 km) snowshoe or ski trek up the summit to the cabin. A sled is on hand for toting supplies—you bring in your own food and sleeping bags.

It's no frills, but it's worth it: This world-class playground has phenomenal backcountry-ski acreage and some of the best rock and ice climbing on the globe. Bookings at the Mountain House are often handled by Don's son Robert and Robert's wife, Marne. Potential renters undergo a minor vetting to check out their "backcountry résumé." (Sample question: "Do you have any crevasse training?") Many who stay in the cabin come with extensive experience in glacier travel, but plenty of others do not; it's recommended that these guests hire guides if they want to do a little glacier exploring.

Windows in five of the cabin's six sides showcase spring and fall's aurora borealis, the crimson alpenglow of summer, and winter's epic snowfalls and pastel sunsets. At night, meteor showers flame across the inky sky. The cabin has books for your reading pleasure, but you may be too busy poring over the volumes of visitor journals going back decades. As one South African visitor wrote, "The 'Little House on the Glacier' has a lot of stories to tell."

OPPOSITE *Pioneering Alaskan bush pilot Don Sheldon built his backcountry cabin atop a nearly 6,000-foot-high (1,829 m) rocky outcrop overlooking Ruth Glacier.*

LEFT *A wooden stairway traces the narrow ledge up to the Sheldon Mountain House.*

BELOW *The cabin can hold up to six people: four on padded sleeping platforms, two in sleeping bags on the floor. A woodstove keeps the place toasty; your only source of fresh water is snow that you shovel into a stockpot to warm up overnight.*

SYÖTE IGLOOS

Glass igloos are a thing in Finland, and for good reason: With its position above the Arctic Circle and wide-open, undeveloped spaces (meaning little to no competition from artificial illumination), this underpopulated region offers primo conditions for viewing the psychedelic night-sky swirls of the aurora borealis.

Though late August to April is the Lapland season for the northern lights, Syöte, the glass igloo atop the Pikku-Syöte fell, offers a panoramic view of the skies year-round, from winter's blazing stars to spring and fall snow showers to the white nights of summer's midnight sun.

On winter evenings, the igloo is nestled in a magical setting of ice-dusted firs and blue-shadow snowbanks. But don't worry about frostbite—thermal glass and underfloor heating will keep you warm and cozy (there's also air-conditioning in summer). The igloo, spacious enough to accommodate two adults and two children, also has a full kitchen; or you can visit the restaurants, bars, and pizza/snack bar at the hotel next door.

Finland's southernmost fell is spectacularly scenic and snow rich—the first flakes fall as early as August. The gentle slopes of Pikku-Syöte and Iso-Syöte are just steps from the igloo and are ideal for children and novices thanks to their array of beginner runs. There are also 75 miles (120 km) of groomed cross-country ski trails. You can chase the northern lights on Canadian snowshoes or cross-country-ski through forests of spruce to a Lappish wilderness hut. Or, for an even more exhilarating adventure, join a husky sled-dog safari, where you can steer the sledge and mush the dogs (the guides show you how) through a snowy landscape of woods and frozen lakes.

The prime aurora seasons here are fall and spring, when nights are cloudless, the cold is not so severe, and disturbances in the earth's magnetic field are at their peak. Of course, the northern lights have their own agenda. Check the local aurora forecasts, and don't sweat it if the light show doesn't appear—you're in the Finnish Lapland, after all, snuggled in a glass igloo pillowed in marshmallow snowdrifts as stars pulse in the night sky.

The glass is thermal and the floor heated, making the igloo bedroom a toasty spot to see the northern lights and stargaze.

Cabanes des Grand
Lacs, page 253

5

WATER

LAKE O'HARA LODGE

Yoho National Park, British Columbia, Canada

It's not easy to snag a room at the Lake O'Hara Lodge. The waiting list has at times stretched into years. In fact, it's such a special place that Parks Canada limits the number of daily and overnight visitors to the area, and since the late 1950s, the only access is via shuttle bus—before that invention, you got there on the back of a horse or your own two feet. But if you can snag a seat on the bus, that restricted access means pristine trails and a truly memorable backcountry experience. And if you're able to book a room at the lodge, all that gorgeous, wild beauty comes with a level of comfort dialed up to 11, gourmet farm-to-table meals, and a wine selection celebrated by *Wine Spectator*.

Built in 1925 by the Canadian Pacific Railway in the heart of the Canadian Rockies, the handsome timber lodge is ringed with lofty green conifers and ice-tipped mountains. Eleven one-bedroom lakeside cabins dot the shore. Each cabin is outfitted with a handcrafted queen bed, a goose-down comforter, and a deck looking out onto the lake. The lodge itself has eight double rooms (with claw-foot tubs); four guide cabins resting on a scenic knoll can accommodate four guests each. Lodge cabins are available mid-June to early October (only lodge rooms are open in the winter cross-country skiing season, January to early April). Rates include all meals and round-trip bus fare, but expect to be truly unplugged here: The lodge has no cell service, Wi-Fi, or TVs. (It does have a popular pay phone.)

The glossy emerald waters of Lake O'Hara mirror the surrounding sweep of rocky peaks and glacial ice. Some of the best hiking trails in Yoho National Park are here, and the lodge provides picnic food and hiking poles and can arrange guided hikes with a certified international mountain guide. Recommended treks include hikes around Lake Oesa, Opabin Lake, and Lake McArthur. In summer, meadows fill with wildflower blooms, and loons float in for a lake skim. After a day exploring the backcountry, take a steam in the lodge's wood-fired sauna. And get your name on the list for next year.

TRUE NORTH CABIN

For years, this dilapidated 1960s-era cabin sat unloved and unlived in, for sale but attracting little interest. The setting was clearly magical: steps from the rocky shoreline of Lake Superior and tucked into a forest of spindly pines, with more than 2 acres (0.8 ha) of hushed wooded privacy. The cabin even came with true Pacific Northwest bona fides: It was built from a Portland house plan, and its lumber was shipped straight from the PNW.

Lynn and Jason Makela saw a real gem through all the disarray. They bought the cabin in 2018, and it took them seven months to complete a thorough remodel. The cabin was blessed with good bones, but the interior was stuck in a fifty-year time warp. Despite the new owners' admiration for its original '60s design chutzpah, some of the worst of the '70s references had to go: Out with bright-orange countertops and flowery wallpaper, in with a white subway-tile backsplash. Brown appliances were replaced with stainless-steel ones, and a

blue bathroom was de-blued. The cabin retains its rustic feel, but sleek modern fixtures and quality appliances give it a real boost in utility. The interior decor leans Scandi-mod, with gleaming hardwood floors, patterned rugs, and a blazing stone fireplace. A coat of sequoia-red paint on the cabin exterior makes it practically hum in a forest of green.

The cabin's name is apt; it just may be the northernmost cabin in Michigan. It's so far north, in fact, that you have a pretty good chance of spotting the aurora borealis on clear evenings from October to April. Meteor showers shoot across the sky in summer. The cabin has 300 feet (91 m) of direct, private shoreline, and at night you can do a little "ship spotting," watching the lights of big freighters gliding along the lake, from the deck. Daytime activities range from hiking nearby Mount Baldy (a 6-mile/9.7 km round trip) to visiting the restaurants, markets, and brewery in the little town of Copper Harbor, just a ten-minute drive away.

The cabin lies on its own private shoreline; you can watch freighters skim the horizon from the renovated deck.

The owners did a complete upgrade on the 1960s-era cabin but retained the big stone fireplace, built with local copper set into the rock face.

CABANES DES GRANDS LACS

How's this for romance: You're tucked into a bed with satiny sheets in a teardrop-shaped treehouse on the edge of a glassy lake. Surrounding the lake is sylvan French countryside—you're within strolling distance of its sweetly scented forests and grazing meadows. All this just a three-and-a-half-hour train ride from the city of love itself, Paris.

The Spa Songe (pictured opposite) is just one of twenty-three fantastical lakeside glamping cabins designed and built by the Coucoo Grands Lacs company in France's Franche-Comté region, bordering Switzerland to the east and the famed French wine region, Burgundy, to the west (the two regions are now merged). Coucoo calls its custom-designed cabins "eco-domains," and the company really takes sustainability to heart. Built of larch and Douglas fir, the cabins are lighted by solar panels and insulated with wool; bathrooms come with dry sawdust toilets. Spa cabins, such as Songe, come with an extra perk: a big Nordic bath, heated to a delicious 104°F (40°C) using a chemical-free purification system.

Spa Songe perches on stilts along the lake's edge. Its first floor holds the bathroom and an open lounge with pillowed built-in seating. A wooden ladder takes you to the second-floor bedroom, with expansive views of the lake that make you feel as if you're floating. If you *really* crave that floating sensation, book one of the Grands Lacs cabins anchored in the middle of the lake. A hundred feet (30 m) from shore, Spa Odyssée, one of the family cabins, can be reached only by boat or pontoon. Another family cabin, Spa Caravelle, is accessed via an 80-foot (24 m) wooden dock.

The Franche-Comté region is one of France's most bucolic, with broad swaths of pristine woods laced with rivers and lakes. Coucoo Grand Lacs' own 200 acres (81 ha) of forest and lakes hold a secure swimming lake (swimming is not permitted in the cabins' lake) and a seasonal outdoor pool.

One of the two bedrooms in the waterside Spa Caravelle family cabin has room for three.

OPPOSITE *Each of Odyssée's two wooden "sleeping balls" is topped with a hairy fringe of thatched straw, giving them the appearance of half-coconuts floating on a wooden raft. An open wood terrace has waterside seating.*

OLIVER LODGE A-FRAME

Barefoot summers on New Hampshire's nearly one thousand lakes and ponds are a cherished tradition, and Oliver Lodge lets you stay in the heart of the state's Lakes Region in boutique style. Built as a hunting lodge in the 1880s, the property has six handsomely outfitted homes set on prime Lake Winnipesaukee beachfront, New Hampshire's grande dame of venerable water holes. On summer days, colorful canoes, kayaks, and paddleboats dot the sandy shore.

One of the Oliver Lodge rentals is a restored early-twentieth-century icehouse, from the days when ice was shaved off the lake and delivered to New England cities by horse-drawn wagons and special ice trains. But folks who want an extra dose of privacy and a chance to experience island living opt for the newer A-Frame, standing tall on a tiny island just 20 feet (6 m) from shore. It's a getaway that's a (very) swimmable distance from the beach, but it comes with two private docks, its own diving board, and a four-person paddleboat to explore Winnipesaukee. Upper and lower mahogany decks wrap around three sides of the cabin, but the views are always facing the waterways. The spacious, sunny living area is open to a fully equipped kitchen. Two upstairs bedrooms, cooled by lake breezes and ceiling fans, have beds enough for six and gorgeous views of the lake.

The lodge offers kayaks and canoes for getting out on the 69-square-mile (179 sq km) spring-fed and crystal-clear Lake Winnipesaukee. It also has a clay tennis court, a horseshoe pit, and firepits for marshmallow roasts under the stars. For motorboat explorations of the lake, you can rent powerboats and pontoons at Meredith Marina. Don't be surprised to see the occasional deer, otter, or mink paddling beside you as you cruise— the local wildlife use the nearly three hundred islands in the lake as seasonal stepping-stones to reach the mainland.

ORCA ISLAND CABINS

See the Alaskan wilderness in all its raw splendor at this private-island eco-resort in Resurrection Bay. Intimate and secluded, the Orca Island Cabins are one of those places that defies pigeonholing. You wouldn't call them backcountry hiking huts, although a gorgeous hike nearby offers breathtaking forest terrain and the reward of a lush waterfall. And they're not a fishing lodge, per se, though gear is provided so that you can angle for meaty rockfish and flounder right off the island's main dock or troll for pink salmon in the house skiff. Rather, they are seven glamping yurts, each sleeping two to four people, with a kitchen, dining, and living room area; a private bathroom with shower; and your own private deck overlooking Humpy Cove.

Yurts are eco-friendly to begin with (they're easy to dismantle and require almost no land development to install), but these ramp up the sustainability factor with solar power and composting toilets.

The 1-acre (0.4 ha) granite island is accessed via water taxi from Seward, an hour-long ride that offers its own stunning scenery. Whether you're sea kayaking in protected Humpy Cove or skimming the glassy waters on a stand-up paddleboard, getting out on the water is certainly a big part of Orca Island's appeal. So is spotting wildlife: Bald eagles fly in for a seafood snack, orcas troll the waters, and entire clans of Steller's sea lions lord over little rock isles.

For a more up-close wildlife experience, noodle around the gin-clear tidal pools in Humpy Cove, the domain of the sunflower starfish, the largest predator starfish in the world—it can grow up to 3 feet (0.9 m) wide. Or sign up for a cruise on Resurrection Bay, where you'll see snowcapped peaks and mountain goats scuttling up the icy hillsides.

Do a deep dive into any or all of these activities, or just kick back to the music of nature in your yurt cabin. At night, wood is provided if you want to make a campfire on the rocks beneath the starry sky. At Orca Island, you write your own wilderness story.

Stand-up paddleboarding is a fun way to get out on the water in Humpy Cove.

OREGON COAST MODERN

The stars were aligned when a couple of Portland creatives became the owners of the 1980s coastal home of the late mid-century architect Marvin Witt. The 1,200-square-foot (111 sq m) treehouse, perched on a woodsy hillside above Manzanita and the crescent beach at Neahkahnie, was an exuberant expression of Pacific Northwest mid-century modern design. Graphic designer Cole Gerst and his wife, Lea Anne, a creative studio director, were smitten. "The creativity and whimsical nature of the architecture shone through," says Cole. "We thought we had found something special." Special, indeed: Witt's work, as *Oregon Home* magazine put it, embodies the mid-century principles of "functionality, natural materials and harmony with the environment."

Built of Douglas fir and cedar, the retro-modern house features three light-filled stories, decks on every floor, and a reverse layout: The top floor is the main living area. The couple chose a simple color palette that reflected the surroundings—soft blue, sand, and a warm yellow—which is echoed in the house's artwork, textiles, and accessories. The only other color is black, which, Cole points out, makes a nice contrast to the original cedar paneling, "and helps the wood be the star of the interior." Bold patterns include a custom Fireclay starburst tile on the kitchen backsplash and Cole's own striking graphic artwork; jazzy Acapulco chairs build on the mid-century theme.

The quarter-moon beach at Neahkahnie is just a five-minute walk down the hill. The Neahkahnie Mountain Viewpoint lies at one of the highest points on the storied Oregon Coast Trail; from the top of the mountain's 1,631-foot (497 m) south peak are incredible views of the Pacific. It's a prime spot for seeing giant gray whales in late December. Famed surf spot Short Sand Beach, aka Shorty's, is a protected cove on the other side of Neahkahnie Mountain and welcomes a daily lineup of surfers and boogie boarders in heavy-duty wet suits. Watch the action, or simply hunt for sand dollars in the tide pools. You're close to a cluster of lively Oregon towns offering fine PNW food and drink. Just be back at the house in time for the evening owl arias.

Each of the cabin's three stories has a deck; from the one on the top floor, you have glimpses of the Pacific Ocean.

LEFT *The coastal cottage was designed with a small footprint, to blend into the natural environment.*

BELOW *This bedspread's pastel patterns echo the energetic lines of the original cedar paneling in the house's third bedroom.*

BIRCHWOOD REDSTONE

Fronted by lake, backed by forest, with sky and water views that go on and on, the Birchwood on Redstone Lake just may be the lake house of your dreams. The setting—overlooking the crystalline waters of Redstone Lake and tucked into 4.5 acres (1.8 ha) of Haliburton Highlands mature birch and pine forest—is hard to beat. The house's elevated perch, the tiered wooden decks, the 250 feet (76 m) of lakeside frontage: pure wow. So when Ryan Harkin and Blair Cox bought the lakefront Ontario house, all they really needed to focus on was the dated interior, where they dialed up the style quotient.

The original elm flooring was sanded down and extended throughout the house. The sun-drenched open-plan living area, with double-height windows and a pitched ceiling finished in pine, got the landed-gentry treatment with a leather sofa and chairs, a seasoned Oriental rug, and vintage Ralph Lauren lamps made of cast iron and American walnut. All three bedrooms got king-size beds dressed in six-hundred-thread-count Egyptian-cotton linens. The result is relaxed boutique living, homey and comfortable as can be.

Outside, steps lead down to three decked lake platforms. The top two decks are so spacious that they are able to hold a table and chairs, loungers, stacks of cut wood, and even a hot tub. A lower deck practically floats on the lake, with a lineup of Adirondack chairs in multiple colors. Another set of steps leads you past exposed rock to the waterfront docking area, where kayaks, paddleboards, and a pedal boat are at the ready for your cruising pleasure. Bring your fishing poles and drop a line in the lake to troll for lake trout, aka Haliburton Gold.

In winter, good skiing is just 16 miles (26 km) away at Sir Sam's Ski/Ride. Haliburton also has some of Ontario's best snow-sledding trails, just minutes from the cottage. Known as the "jewel of Haliburton," the main attraction, Redstone Lake, is "crystal-clear and the cleanest water you can find," Harkin says. The lake freezes over completely in winter, and you can stroll or snowmobile on it. Or you can just stare at the serene vista from the deck of your elevated getaway home.

One of three decks with tree-fringed views of the "jewel of Haliburton": crystal-clear Redstone Lake.

Birchwood's high-ceilinged living area is flooded with light from sliding glass doors, framed windows, and skylights.

EMERALD LAKE LODGE

Yoho National Park,
British Columbia,
Canada

Emerald Lake Lodge dates back to 1902, and the hand-hewn timber exterior wears its patina well. It doesn't hurt that the surrounding mountainscape and icy blue lakes of Yoho National Park remain little changed from the rough-and-ready 1880s. That's probably thanks to the whims of Canada's first prime minister, John A. Macdonald, who created the park in 1886 after being thunderstruck by the beauty of the Rockies during his ride on the newly completed Transcontinental Railroad.

The lodge sits on 13 acres (5.3 ha) of gorgeous mountain wilderness; it's the lake's lone property. The twenty-four cabin buildings share the lodge's rustic exterior, but inside, it's all about contemporary comfort. The eighty-five rooms and suites come with wood-burning fieldstone fireplaces, feather duvets, and private balconies. The Point Cabin suite has a wraparound balcony overlooking the lake. What the rooms *don't* have are TVs, cell service, AC, or Wi-Fi (you can log on in the lodge). The turn-back-the-clock vibe includes a century-old stone fireplace and an oak bar salvaged from an 1890s Yukon saloon. The Mount Burgess Dining

Room food, though, is no throwback; you will dine very well on the refined Rocky Mountain cuisine. The menu is farm to table—or in this case, prairie to table—showcasing humanely raised game meat from the lodge's own Calgary ranch. A charcuterie plate lists such delicacies as elk salami, air-dried bison, and wild boar pâté.

The lodge connects you to a world of wilderness recreation, offering opportunities to snowboard, dogsled, and both downhill and cross-country ski. Summertime pleasures include biking, canoeing, and white-water rafting. Hikes from the lodge take you to falls, alpine lakes, colorful hoodoos, even a mountain teahouse or two. A flat 3-mile (4.8 km) trail circumnavigating the lake makes a leisurely trek on foot, snowshoes, or cross-country skis.

Between two of the mountains that border Emerald Lake is one of the most important fossil finds in the world. The Cambrian creatures in Burgess Shale were buried in a mud avalanche half a billion years ago, leaving skeletal remains in finely etched detail. You can visit the site by guided tour from July to September.

BIG BEAR A-FRAME

When SoCal swelters, Big Bear Lake makes for a cool getaway in the heart of the San Bernardino National Forest. Fed by mountain snowfall, this crystalline alpine lake is a recreational powerhouse, home to excellent fishing (for trout and bass), snowboarding, skiing, swimming, hiking, and mountain biking. Enjoy all the area has to offer with a stay in one of Big Bear's most desirable cabins, tucked into an 8,000-square-foot (743 sq m) forest cul-de-sac scented with pine. It's romantic *and* family-friendly, an ideal spot for getting to the ski slopes, trekking serious mountain trails, or just staying warm and cozy in your cabin in the woods.

And this A-frame was *built* for warmth and coziness. The interior oozes earthy masculinity, with a big leather couch the color of cognac, a sleek black wood-burning stove, and wooden walls and floors stained in dark hues. With big windows and a skylight, it practically glows from within—you'll want to snuggle in and never leave. The kitchen has a gleaming stainless-steel oven, and upstairs is a sprawling loft with a beanbag nook and a record player on one side and a queen bed and two twin beds on the other. Decks upstairs and down are for sitting and sipping, and a set of Lincoln Logs makes the perfect kiddie distraction.

The Big Bear Lake area has a retro, summer-camp appeal. But even Big Bear first-timers may experience a sense of déjà vu when they visit. That's because they've probably seen it on the big screen: Since the 1920s, Big Bear's crystal-clear skies and multifaceted terrain have made it a favorite natural back lot for Hollywood films and television shows—including *Heidi*, starring Shirley Temple, and *Old Yeller*. That ever-shifting landscape will have you in hushed mountain forest one minute and Joshua Tree–like desert brush in another. The high elevation means plenty of winter snow for skiing and snowboarding at nearby Big Bear Mountain Resort. In summer, lake temperatures are brisk, but there are designated swimming spots, like West Shore Beach.

The generously sized loft has room for three beds and a beanbag nook for listening to music or solitary reading.

OPPOSITE *Stained-wood walls and floors, beams painted black, and a cognac-hued couch give the cabin what the owner calls a moody "cigar bar" feel.*

Å AUGE CAMP

Norwegians are big believers in living the *friluftsliv* lifestyle—being outdoors and in nature, regardless of the weather. The outdoor life makes Nords happy, and it shows: As *National Geographic* reports, Norway and its major cities constantly nab high marks in the United Nations' World Happiness Report. To get a dose of friluftsliv for yourself, head to Å Auge ("River Eye") camp. Set on the banks of the rushing Tessungåe River, the complex of tents and cabins—deep in forest backcountry and way off the grid—was built so people can experience nature in what the camp calls an "authentic, simple, and inexpensive way," no matter the season. Just the way Norwegians like it.

To truly immerse yourself, stay in the handcrafted treehouse that sits 20 feet (6 m) off the ground; its large windows face the river, and skylights open to the stars (in summer, bring a sleep mask to block out the midnight sun!). The cabin is surprisingly luxurious and sturdily insulated, with comfy mattresses and wool blankets, a full kitchen, and a wood-fired stove to keep things toasty. A covered front deck looks out on the river and its banks of tall spruce and pine.

The complex uses no electricity, only candles and solar lamps. It has no running water, either, but that's just an opportunity to take a delicious bush bath in one of the big tubs along the river. You simply fill the tub with buckets of pristine river water, light a fire (wood is provided), and wait for your bath to heat up the natural way. A good hot soak beside a rushing river is sure to cure whatever ails you.

The Å Auge Camp is close to great hiking, kayaking, and fishing (for arctic char and river trout). You can go cross-country-skiing in nearby Hardangervidda National Park or forage for mushrooms or wild blueberries in the woods surrounding the camp. Or you can take a leisurely swim in the Tessungåe. Whatever you do, you'll be communing with nature, Norwegian friluftsliv-style.

Wall-size windows in the handcrafted treehouse look onto the rock-strewn Tessungåe River and Norwegian forestland.

PUMPHOUSE POINT

**Lake Saint Clair,
Tasmania,
Australia**

The icy blue waters of Lake Saint Clair, Australia's deepest lake, are rimmed by a highlands wilderness of button grass plains and myrtle forests. The country's top bushwalking trek, the Overland Track, meanders 40 miles (64 km) over stunning alpine terrain right to the lake's edge. But back in the 1940s, engineers caught up in the frenzy of industrialization decided to turn this gorgeous lake into a hydroelectric power source. At the end of a jetty stretching 820 feet (250 m) into Lake Saint Clair, they built a five-story pumphouse with massive water turbines for delivering water to the nearest power station.

It was an interesting idea, but the constant damming and pumping of the lake led to fluctuating water levels, which in turn led to environmental mayhem. Banks eroded; trees drowned. And the need for a hydroelectric pumphouse proved . . . underwhelming. Today, after decades in hibernation, the ninety-year-old pumphouse has found new life as the heart of the Pumphouse Point wilderness retreat. A smashing gut redesign inside installed twelve smartly contemporary rooms and lounges with fireplaces and honor bars. The building's industrial heritage shines through in the concrete floors, copper piping, and steel-framed windows. The old lakeside substation has also been revamped, with six resort rooms. But the most impressive lodging at Pumphouse Point just may be the freestanding cabin suite tucked along the Saint Clair shoreline. The Retreat includes a fabulous covered outdoor pavilion and a soaking tub in the bush.

The Pumphouse restaurant serves upscale farmhouse fare, Tasmanian craft beer, and regional pinot. E-bikes, mountain bikes, and rowboats are at hand for the kid in you (note: actual kids aren't allowed). The lake is now part of the Tasmanian Wilderness World Heritage Area, and the hiking here is world class, with some 62 miles (100 km) of walks into a biodiverse terrain of eucalypt forest and rain-forest ferns. Fly-fishing the lake for Tasmanian trout is epic. Pumphouse Point is also home to wild fauna of the Tassie variety, including wallabies, Tasmanian devils, and platypuses.

Just steps from the Retreat is a deep soaking tub for private alfresco bathing.

OPPOSITE The Retreat bedroom has a ceiling and walls of Tasmanian oak and is outfitted in locally crafted furniture and ceramics.

RIVIÈRE CABIN

The classic cabin in the woods has been scaled up and totally kitted out at the Rivière Cabin near Mont-Tremblant, Quebec. The cabin is located not only in the forested hills and folds of the recreation-rich Laurentian Mountains but also just steps from the smooth-flowing streams of Devil's River, and it comes with its own private swimming platform, kayaks, and stand-up paddleboard for summertime dipping and cruising.

The Rivière Cabin stretches to nearly 2,200 square feet (204 sq m), with four bedrooms over two stories, a full cooking kitchen, and room enough for ten people to really sprawl. The vibe inside is warm and embracing, with rustic knotty-pine walls and a cozy conversation pit made up of three couches. A stone wood-burning fireplace blazes in the living room. There's even a piano for inspired tinkling (and no neighbors to complain about the noise). Handmade wood chairs line a large dining room table. Outside is a firepit with a circle of Muskoka chairs and a hot tub under the stars.

The cabin is surrounded by big firs and cedars. Take a skim on Devil's River in one of the house kayaks, passing a forest of silver maples and the bearded rock face of La Vache Noire mountain. The waters are sparkling and clear, the river bottom a gorgeous mosaic of well-worn stones. Disembark at Sand Island, a private spit of sand about a half mile (800 m) up the river, for an idyllic picnic. Devil's River is a fine fly-casting destination, where anglers troll for speckled river trout. You're also just a ten-minute drive to Mont-Tremblant National Park and its 583 square miles (1,510 sq km) of recreational parkland, from hiking and mountain-bike trails to sheer rock for daredevil climbing.

When winter comes, however, it's all about the powder. You're just a three-minute drive to the Tremblant ski resort, for blissful days of skiing (downhill and cross-country), snowboarding, ice fishing, dogsledding, and snowshoeing. Then it's off to the Scandinave Spa Mont-Tremblant, where steamy baths and thermal waterfalls help get the kinks out. And winter or summer, it's always fun to visit nearby Parc Omega (home to another great place to stay—see page 89). Embark on the self-driven safari to feed carrots to reindeer, spot the park's pack of gray wolves, and say hello to the resident moose.

THE POND HOUSE

It's only an eighty-minute drive from the urban wilds of Manhattan, but the Pond House gets you out of your city head fast. From afar, the cabin has the no-nonsense look of a little red schoolhouse of yore, but here the full-bodied bones are weathered steel and blackened cedar. Step inside and you're greeted by an airy, expansive great room, grounded by a cool concrete floor. Many of the furnishings were built with the wood of old sugar maples once left to languish on the pond shores. Four seasons of sunlight pour in through big glass doors and windows, framed just so to showcase the leaf-dappled pond and the green fringe of forest beyond.

Custom designed by its owner, a Brooklyn architect, as a woodsy retreat for his young family, the chapel-like Pond House seamlessly meshes with its natural environment. The decor is reclaimed-meets-modern-utilitarian: Ash trees weakened by borer beetles on the property have been carved into chunky stools (kids love them), while the twenty-first-century woodstove comes with sleek, supermodel lines. The overall effect, inside and out, is pared down and unshowy. This "haiku of a home," as the New York Times called it, provides the ultimate luxury in quiet and seclusion.

The house can hold up to six people—three small bedrooms are tucked away in a modest extension—but the locus of the house is the great room with its views of pond and forest and the occasional deer or wild turkey. The pond is fed by a tumbling waterfall, and it's all yours. Take a dip in the silky waters or wander the wooded property's 19 acres (7.7 ha) among old stone fences and wetlands. In summer, the house is ringed in native grasses and wildflowers and a sonic symphony of crickets and bullfrogs; in winter, the snowy landscape is ripe for exploring by snowshoes.

In the evening, light the firepit under a sky blazing with stars and gaze back at the cathedral glow of the cabin: The hustle of the city will feel light-years away.

The Pond House's sunlit living area has direct views of the pond. Note the stubby wood stools, carved from one of the property's ash trees.

OPPOSITE The custom-designed exterior features weathered steel and blackened cedar.

RIVER CABAAN

When Portland couple Karie Higgins and Lee Gibson fell for a run-down 1963 riverside fishing cabin in 2017, there was a lot to love. It had 328 feet (100 m) of private river frontage and stood on 4 acres (1.6 ha) of towering firs and hardwoods. A long deck overlooked a gentle slope of wildflowers and the sparkling green Wilson River below. The foundation was solid, but dark wood paneling in every room gave the house a closed-in feel. So the couple swept in, covering the walls, floors, and beams—even the big brick fireplace—with a blizzard of white paint. Today everything looks and feels roomier. Sunlight streams in from wall-to-wall windows in the living area and bounces off all that dazzling white.

Higgins and Gibson did more than apply paint to open up the space, though. They ripped out dark kitchen cabinets and replaced them with floating oak shelving. They built a birch-ply bench that they tucked into the dining nook's bay window. Throw in the cabin's mid-century modern furnishings, and it's as if Palm Springs jetted in to gray Oregon and set up house.

The River Cabaan lies in a secluded setting just ten minutes from Tillamook and one hour from Portland by car. It's an hour's drive to classic Oregon beaches like Cannon and Short Sand and a thirty-minute drive to Cape Lookout State Park, where a 5-mile (8 km) round-trip hike offers you the chance to spot whales on the ocean horizon.

But you don't even have to leave the comforts of the cabin to enjoy the pleasures of the Oregon outdoors: From the cabin deck (which has a table and lounge chairs and is strung with sparkly lights), a set of metal steps leads down to the river, where you can swim in the gentle currents. The house provides inflatable boats for long, leisurely floats in rock-strewn streams, and you can fish right from the shore. Or maybe you'll opt to light a campfire on the pebbled beach for true blue-hour bliss.

The gentle currents of
the Wilson River meander
alongside the cabin amid
stands of towering Oregon
evergreens.

The open living area is lean but layered with texture, and bright with floor-to-ceiling white, from the fuzzy shag rug to a fireplace painted brilliant ivory.

CAMP WANDAWEGA

Camp Wandawega was built on a bedrock of ill repute: It was born a bootlegger's lair in 1925 and smoothly segued into a brothel, gambling joint, and hideout for bums on the run. It wasn't until 1951 that a nice Polish family from Chicago turned the 25-acre (10 ha) camp into a legitimate middlebrow lakeside resort (with a bar, natch). In the 1970s, it became a retreat for Catholic Latvians, who sponsored a lakeside kids' camp in the summer months. A young boy named David Hernandez and his family spent idyllic summers here. Some thirty years later, that boy bought his childhood getaway.

Hernandez and his wife, Tereasa Surratt, leaped straight over Wandawega's bawdy past to create an homage to wholesome summer camp life, sprinkled with some Wes Anderson pixie-dust whimsy. The camp's homespun activities—archery, canoeing, horseshoes, fishing, and hiking—celebrate the simple pleasures of the outdoors, circa 1955. We're talking campfires and s'mores, vintage bikes and cane fishing rods. Guests have access to the private beach and woods, an outdoor grill and an old smoker, sports courts, and boats—but, unlike at real camp, the schedule is utterly freestyle. In winter months, three of the cabins remain open for guests, who can access trails for cross-country skiing and snowshoeing.

Camp Wandawega is made for groups and families. The range of accommodations is myriad and delightful, from an honest-to-gosh tepee to a "canned ham": a vintage aluminum trailer. Cabins include Cedar, an updated original from the 1950s resort days, with a bright, whitewashed interior and a wrought-iron bed. Named for the dreamy vista from its sunporch, the three-bedroom Lakeview Cabin is another mid-century original; walls hung with vintage tennis rackets and college banners give it a time-warp feel. The Treehouse is a fantastical communal clubhouse built around a massive elm tree hung with swings and hammocks. The Stockroom Bar is vintage piled on vintage, complete with a Prohibition-era padlock. The camp's original speakeasy, the Lodge, has an authentic whiskey-soaked vibe, with fat leather sofas and bearskin rugs.

The whitewashed interior of the Cedar Cabin is done up with vintage photos, a straw mat, and a nubby bedspread in rainbow stripes.

OPPOSITE *The camp's original guest rooming house, the three-level Bunk House was built into a tree-shaded hillside along the lake's edge.*

The simple pleasures of summertime lake life include doing cannonballs off the camp dock.

At Wandawega, old-school doesn't necessarily mean camp latrines and group showers (although they're here, too). This pretty Bunk House bath features a freestanding tub and shower.

TOP BUNKHOUSE

*Vintage paddles add to the
time-warp feel of Wandawega,
plus they still do the hard work
on canoe jaunts.*

BORA BORÉAL

For those who've had fantasies of houseboat living but are less keen on voyaging than simply feeling the float, this cottage is a dream. Bora Boréal levitates on the surface of a glassy lake, but it isn't going anywhere. Why should it? It's got the best perch on the lake, ringed by scene-stealing forest evergreens climbing tall, snowy peaks. Windows in myriad shapes and sizes let in the views, and a glass garage door (yes, a garage door) makes a perfect wall-size window. The Quebecois architect/owner, Nicolas Robitaille, designed the floating cottage with architect Danielle Hébert-Boutin as an immersive way to experience nature in modern-rustic comfort "so people would be in a chic living room and at the same time feel the natural wildness of living on water," Robitaille says. "The all-glass garage door was integrated into this mindset."

The houseboat's light-filled interior is smartly stylish. It's got a chic minimalist design, all natural woods and clean lines. You're warmed by a big black woodstove in the living area and surrounded by walls of stained pine. A sofa and chairs beckon with mid-century curves. The palette throughout is earthy browns and blacks, other than the pop of a saffron-yellow armchair and the dazzle of five Turkish mosaic glass lamps in the dining nook. A built-in wood banquette topped by black cushions traces the kitchen walls. The sunlit bedroom upstairs is reached by a pull-down ladder, and horizontal windows showcase the mountain greenery. A firepit outside is made for cool nights under star-spangled skies.

This pocket of seclusion and tranquility is on a private estate just a thirty-minute drive from downtown Quebec City. Warm-weather activities include walking on trails, fishing, and swimming at a sandy beach a minute's walk away. Kayaks and stand-up paddleboards are available for skimming the lake, and you're close to Sentiers du Moulin and its exceptional hiking and mountain biking trails. In winter, snowshoes are provided for exploring the woods around the cabin; be sure to bring your skates to trace icy figure eights on the frozen lake.

A thick aluminum frame affixed with special PVC floats firmly maintains the cabin's ballast and stability.

THE *JAMES FRANCO* HOUSEBOAT

In the extreme eastern corner of Queens, New York, are the Rockaways: a little bit of SoCal set down in small-town Atlantic beach sand. We're talking taco stands and arty shops and surfer dive bars. Yes, you can surf tasty waves in New York City. At the same time, an old-school boardwalk and clackety subway trains remind you that you're still in the Big Apple.

In a gated marina just two blocks from Rockaway Beach floats the *James Franco*, a quirky little riverboat and a labor of love. The decor aboard is shabby-chic clutter with nautical and tiki-bar references. The blue-painted shell of a horseshoe crab hangs on a wall. Surfboards and fishing poles line the ceiling. The upper deck, strung with fairy lights, offers spacious seating and views of planes going in and out of JFK airport.

Unlike most boats at the marina, the *James Franco* has an actual bathroom, but the zero-flush toilet system has limited flushes and the shower limited hot water (marina toilets are available). The kitchen is fully equipped and has an off-grid gas stove; you can also barbecue on the lower-porch grill. The bedroom is seriously comfortable—and the whole boat has AC! As one guest put it, this is one rad pad.

No, it's not a cabin, but it has the spirit of one—a stay on the *James Franco* is a singular adventure. Two longboards on the side of the boat are yours to use in sampling the brisk Atlantic surf. Cleaner New York Harbor waters mean a good chance of spotting humpback whales breaching on the horizon while you're lazing on the beach. Rental bikes are available for noodling around the Rockaways. Or just relax on the gently rocking deck, breathe in that salty air, and earn your sea legs.

Meditate on the surfboard hanging from the ceiling as you drift off to sleep in the boat's surprisingly roomy and ultracomfortable bedroom.

OPPOSITE *The cabin is a flavorful mash-up of colorful pillows and the kinds of knickknacks you might pick up at a sea captain's yard sale—including table legs made of driftwood and an anchor lamp.*

WILLOW TREEHOUSE

It's been called a spaceship on stilts and an architectural dream. Its designer, British architect Antony Gibbon, called the style a potent mix of "geometric, rustic, modern, glamping." Tucked into trees on 34 acres (14 ha) of bucolic Catskills woods just a two-hour drive from New York City, the Willow Treehouse is so high off the ground—held aloft by a single pair of angled metal beams—it seems to float above the pond. Gibbon is famed for taking treehouse design to the literal heights. His conceptual treehouse designs are thrilling examples of biomimicry: emulating the elements and designs of nature to better mesh with the natural environment, with an eye toward more sustainable design. He has said that his goal is "making the architectural environment work into nature as opposed to the other way around."

The Willow Treehouse is clad in Catskills-sourced reclaimed cedar that blends handsomely into the wooded surrounds. The modern interior is designed for ultimate comfort. The open-plan space is airy and uncluttered, with walls of warm reclaimed pine. In the kitchen, a wood island has a solid concrete countertop and a big farmhouse sink. A ladder leads to an open sleeping loft, where the pitched wood ceiling and glass walls on either side slope upward; skylights bring in even more light. A "chill room" at the back of the treehouse is a glass-and-wood nook with floor cushions for watching deer, rabbits, and even black bears on the ground below.

The design uses every opportunity to bring the outdoors in: The window in the living area, with an unobstructed view of the pond, takes up practically the entire wall, and more windows on either side have you floating in green. Under the cabin is a spacious cedar deck, and closer to the (very swimmable) pond is a Swedish hot tub that you heat up with firewood. If you feel the need for a little more action, the legendary town of Woodstock is just a fifteen-minute drive from the house. It's charming and full of quaint boho shops and fine restaurants, and fully embodies the Willow Treehouse spirit of living the good life amid natural surrounds.

In the living area, a picture window the size of the wall looks out onto the pond.

OPPOSITE *Willow Treehouse is built of locally sourced, reclaimed cedar and is held aloft by a pair of angled metal beams, with a cedar deck underneath.*

The cabin was fashioned
to emulate the designs of
nature and mesh with the
native environment of these
Catskills woods.

*Zion Eco-Cabin,
page 331*

Desert

6

THE JOSHUA TREE FOLLY

This stunning two-cabin home is the work of architect Malek Alqadi, who built it in the footprint of an abandoned 1954 homestead. Using materials either salvaged from the original structure or locally sourced, Alqadi devised a pared-down, modern design with an old soul. In looks and attitude, the cabins recall both the iconic red barn and the stark landscape aesthetic of artists like Donald Judd. You're way off the grid and solar dependent here (Wi-Fi, air-conditioning, and lights are all sustainably powered) yet totally plugged into smart-home technology, where controls work the locks, window screens, and Bluetooth music system.

Clad in heavy-duty IronOx steel, the cabins already show a time-rusted patina. Folly is built around indoor-outdoor livability—a reasonable proposition in a dry desert environment with 282 sunny days a year and little rain or humidity. A lighted ladder shimmies up the side of the smaller cabin to the alfresco stargazing loft, where you can sleep in a dreamy heated bed under twinkling night skies. A galvanized metal trough used to feed cattle has been repurposed as a refreshing plunge pool on the outdoor deck. A rainfall shower has floor-to-ceiling glass windows for unfiltered desert views. At night, you can tell ghost stories around the outdoor firepit (wood provided); during the day, hammocks are at the ready for breezy sunbaths.

Interiors of locally milled, unvarnished plywood play off walls painted in gradating hues of deep blue and green, like the chiaroscuro ripple of lake water. Concrete floors and a concrete kitchen backsplash are softened by textiles and curved-edge furnishings. A compact kitchen has a two-burner stovetop. The entire property is carbon neutral; even the Silvon bedsheets are chemical-free and "oligodynamic"—sheet fibers have been fused with natural silver to deter bacterial growth.

On the fringes of Joshua Tree National Park, these rust-red A-frames make a mighty bold statement against a high-desert backdrop. Joshua Tree's incredible desert ecosystem is just an eight-minute drive from the property. It's a landscape full of surprises—like roadrunners and rare desert tortoises, green palm-tree oases, and a June bloom of desert wildflowers.

The burly humps and folds of the Bullion Mountains dominate the horizon.

OPPOSITE The rust-red A-frames are off the grid and surrounded by rugged peaks and desert scrub brush.

TAOS GOJI ECO LODGE

San Cristobal,
New Mexico

An overnight at the Taos Goji Eco Lodge is not your everyday farm stay. Yes, there are barn cats and roosters, baskets of fresh eggs in pastel shades, and a roaming donkey or two. But the main focus of this organic flower and vegetable farm is the bright-red "superfruit" known as the goji berry, prized for its nutritious, antioxidant qualities. At this 40-acre (16 ha) high-desert retreat, guests stay in rustic hundred-year-old log-and-adobe cabins shaded by cottonwoods, with interiors that up the style quotient with Southwestern rugs, stained wood beams, and local pottery. Visitors are invited to take a soak in the Japanese cedar *ofuro* (hot tub) or meditate in the big tepee in the woods.

It's no surprise that this historic farm has an artful, bohemian soul: It's just around the bend from the town of Taos, at the foot of the breathtaking Sangre de Cristo Mountains. Despite a population of just six thousand residents, Taos has long had an outsize presence in the arts world, incubating world-renowned artist colonies and drawing luminaries like writer D. H. Lawrence.

The farm has its own rich history: In the Huxley Cabin, you can sleep in the very house where *Brave New World* novelist Aldous Huxley lived and wrote in the 1930s. (He even built the outhouse facilities, still standing.) The 500-square-foot (46 sq m) cabin has its own fully equipped kitchen and room enough to sleep four. Whitewashed walls serve as a striking contrast to the beamed ceiling and wood floors, while textiles in native Southwestern patterns provide pops of color.

Like the artists and writers who used this countryside as a beautiful retreat, guests will find plenty of natural attractions to inspire them. You're just 11 miles (18 km) from Taos and only 23 miles (37 km) from the legendary ski runs of the Taos ski valley. Just north of Taos, you can take a hot soak in mud-bottomed Black Rock Hot Springs. The farm is surrounded by Carson National Forest, and the night skies here are lit up in Milky Way stardust.

In the 1930s, the cabin was rustic and remote and lacked plumbing, but writer Aldous Huxley found the landscape so inspiring, he settled in for a while.

DOME IN THE DESERT

When Los Angelenos Kathrin and Brian Smirke bought the little geodesic dome near the town of Joshua Tree, it was a mess, with sad carpeting, dark 1980s-era paneling, and a dilapidated kitchen. The couple had been on the hunt for a weekend retreat from the city when they saw something in the dome that inspired them. One big plus was a secluded setting on more than 2 acres (0.8 ha) of serene, wild Mojave terrain, with high-desert peaks on the horizon. The location was dreamy; the dome would need a major overhaul to match the idyllic surrounds.

The Smirkes are multihyphenates, designers and developers and DIYers, but even with their versatile skills, they couldn't expedite the reno, which took nine months. Today all that dark matter is gone, replaced by a sunny, sprightly two-bedroom home mixing Palm Springs chic and desert bohemian style. The geodesic walls give the rooms an origami dimensionality, and ceilings reaching up to 16 feet (4.9 m) make the space feel lofty and create serious acoustics for belting out your favorite songs.

A much-needed roof renovation was a good opportunity to add five skylights, and whitewashed walls reflect the sunlight pouring in. Sticking to a strict budget, the couple outfitted the place in Craigslist finds and wasted nothing, creating artwork and furnishings out of scraps. Bookends were made from fence posts, a side table was crafted from tree stumps, and leftover wood triangles became wall decor. Artisanal crafts like the beautiful macramé wall hangings from Janelle Pietrzak, blankets with tribal prints, and vintage kilim pillows add even more bohemian flavor.

The dome is about a half mile (0.8 km) from the nearest neighbor, but you're just a few minutes' drive from the cafés, boutiques, and museums of Joshua Tree (including the tiny World Famous Crochet Museum). You're also close to Joshua Tree National Park, a sprawling desert wilderness with popular hiking trails and rock-climbing routes. In the evenings, comfy chairs outside the dome let you gaze up into pollution-free starry skies.

Sunlight floods into the whitewashed main living area through windows and five skylights. The dome shape gives the interior a lofty feel.

ZION ECO-CABIN

The Zion Eco-Cabin faces the southern flank of the Zion mountains, federally protected land known as the Canaan Mountain Wilderness. Inside the mini A-frame is a compact solar-powered studio space with a comfy king-size bed, a couple of nightstands, and not much else. But this little suitcase of an A-frame unpacks in delightful fashion: A hinged glass wall pops up, flip-phone-style, to open the space to a panorama of rainbow-hued bluffs and mesas, with nothing but desert sagebrush in between. You can lie in bed and gaze out at pastel cliffs of rippled sandstone rock. Shut the glass wall at night to a dreamscape of black hills and Milky Way skies.

"The cabin was designed to be an experience of nature," says owner Mindy Barlow. "The question was how to straddle the line between comfort, connection, and minimal environmental impact. This design gave us the best of all worlds."

An observation deck just steps from the cabin holds a grill, a table, and tiki torches; after dinner, you can warm up around the stone firepit and stare deep into the galaxies.

With ten months of sunshine and cornflower-blue skies, southern Utah is a four-season destination. Yes, winters can be cold and summers three-digit hot. But thick blankets and a portable heater keep you snug on chilly nights, and even the hottest days often cool down at night.

Zion National Park, the fourth most visited national park in the country, is less than an hour's drive from the cabin, and a hike into its storied canyonlands (or the free shuttle ride on the park's Scenic Drive) is a must. But you're also a short drive away from less-trammeled desert gems, like the red-rock cliffs and juniper trees of Water Canyon, a ten-minute drive from the cabin— Mindy's favorite local hike. "It gives you the feel of being in Zion without the crowds," she says. The cabin is also a ten-minute drive from Edge of the World Brewery, where you can sample craft beers and some seriously good pizza against a backdrop of craggy vermilion cliffs.

The cabin offers easy access to the spectacular red-rock Zion canyonlands.

CABIN DIRECTORY

Included below are the rental websites and Instagram handles (where applicable) for each property that appears in the book, in alphabetical order. More detailed information on the accommodations is also provided, including if the property is pet-friendly and what recreational activities are available in the area.

👣	**HIKING**
⛰	**MOUNTAIN SPORTS** Mountain biking and/or climbing
❄	**SNOW SPORTS** Cross-country skiing, downhill skiing, snowboarding, and/or snowshoeing
🌊	**WATER SPORTS** Boating, canoeing, fishing, kayaking, and/or swimming

Å AUGE CAMP [page 277]
Tinn, Telemark, Norway
aacamp.no | @aa_camp
Accommodates 2–9 | Pets welcome

ALPENGLOW CABIN [page 138]
Twin Lakes, Colorado
airbnb.com/rooms/36174093
@alpenglowcabin
Accommodates 6

ALPINE LAKES HIGH CAMP
[page 173]
Leavenworth, Washington State
alpinelakeshighcamp.com
@alpine_lakes_high_camp
Accommodates 2–10 | Pets welcome

BIG BEAR A-FRAME [page 272]
Big Bear Lake, California
bigbearaframe.com
@whiskeyridgechalet
Accommodates 4

BIRCHWOOD REDSTONE

(page 266)
Haliburton, Ontario, Canada
airbnb.ca/rooms/32042299
@thebirchwoodcottageco
Accommodates 6 | Pets welcome

A BLACK A-FRAME (page 30)

Kerhonkson, New York
airbnb.com/rooms/44195397
@ablackaframe
Accommodates 4

BOLT FARM TREEHOUSE (page 33)

Wadmalaw Island, South Carolina
boltfarmtreehouse.com
@boltfarmtreehouse
Accommodates 2

BONNIE BELLE CABIN (page 151)

Silverton, Colorado
bonniebellecabin.com
@bonniebellecabin
Accommodates 8

BORA BORÉAL (page 303)

Sainte-Brigitte-de-Laval, Quebec,
    Canada
airbnb.com/rooms/44188654
@boraborealqc
Accommodates 4 | Pets welcome

THE BOX HOP (page 18)

Rockbridge, Ohio
airbnb.com/users/show/194261977
@theboxhop
Accommodates 6

CABANES DES GRANDS LACS

(page 253)
Franche-Comté, France
cabanesdesgrandslacs.com
@coucoocabanes
Accommodates 2–6 | Pets welcome

CAMP WANDAWEGA (page 294)

Elkhorn, Wisconsin
wandawega.com
@campwandawega
Accommodates 2–24

CAMPWELL WOODS (page 40)

Cherry Wood, Bath, England
campwell.co.uk
@campwell.woods
Accommodates 2–3

CASA ALICE (page 124)

Rio Grande, Puerto Rico
airbnb.com/rooms/42646108
@casa_alicepr
Accommodates 7 | Pets welcome

DOME IN THE DESERT (page 326)

Joshua Tree, California
airbnb.com/rooms/plus/2093755
@domeinthedesert
Accommodates: 4

DUNTON HOT SPRINGS (page 183)

Dolores, Colorado
duntondestinations.com
@duntonhotsprings
Accommodates 2–8 | Pets welcome

EASTERN THREDBO CEDAR CABIN (page 146)

Thredbo Village, New South Wales,
    Australia
theeasternthredbovillage.com
@theeasternthredbovillage
Accommodates 2

ECOCAMP PATAGONIA (page 174)

Torres del Paine National Park,
    Patagonia, Chile
ecocamp.travel | @ecocamp
Accommodates 2–4

EMERALD LAKE LODGE (page 271)

Yoho National Park, British Columbia,
    Canada
crmr.com/resorts/emerald-lake
@emeraldlakelodge
Accommodates 2–4 | Pets welcome

FARAWAY TREEHOUSE (page 59)

Cumbria, England
canopyandstars.co.uk
@canopyandstars
Accommodates 4

FERN GULLY CABINS (page 98)

Jordan River, British Columbia, Canada
airbnb.com/users/show/161052410
@ferngullycabins
Accommodates 3

FIRVALE WILDERNESS CAMP (page 154)

Bella Coola Valley, British Columbia,
    Canada
firvalewildernesscamp.com
@firvale_wilderness_camp
Accommodates 2–4

GETAWAY FRAME (page 26)

Pinetop-Lakeside, Arizona
airbnb.com/rooms/23303692
@getawayframe
Accommodates 13

GETAWAY (page 56)

Locations available near Atlanta, Austin, Boston, Charlotte, Cleveland, Dallas, Houston, Los Angeles, New York City, Pittsburgh, Portland (OR), Raleigh, San Antonio, and Washington, DC
getaway.house | @getawayhouse
Accommodates 2–4 | Pets welcome

GREY DUCK CABIN (page 83)

Finland, Minnesota
greyduckcabin.com | @greyduckcabin
Accommodates 4 | Pets welcome

HATCHER PASS LODGE (page 145)

Palmer, Alaska
hatcherpasslodge.com
@hatcherpasslodge
Accommodates 1–6 | Pets welcome

HATTVIKA LODGE (page 226)

Ballstad, Lofoten Islands, Norway
hattvikalodge.no | @hattvikalodge
Accommodates 2–6

HERGEST LEE CABIN (page 104)

Burlingjobb, Wales
hergest-lee.com | @hergest_lee
Accommodates 5 | Pets welcome

HIDEOUT BALI (page 127)

Selat, Bali, Indonesia
hideoutbali.com | @hideoutbali
Accommodates 2–4

HIGH COUNTRY CABIN (page 208)

Ben Ohau, Pukaki Ward, New Zealand
highcountrycabin.co.nz
@highcountrycabin
Accommodates 5

HINTERHOUSE (page 167)

La Conception, Quebec, Canada
hintercompany.com | @hintercompany
Accommodates 4

THE HUNTER GREENHOUSE (page 92)

Tannersville, New York
thehunterhouses.co
@thehunterhouses
Accommodates 6

IDYLLCREEK A-FRAME (page 222)

Idyllwild, California
experienceidyllwild.com
@experienceidyllwild
Accommodates 6 | Pets welcome

THE *JAMES FRANCO* HOUSEBOAT (page 306)
Queens, New York
airbnb.com/rooms/12272376
Accommodates 2

JOFFRE CREEK CABINS
(page 189)
Pemberton, British Columbia, Canada
joffrecreekcabins.ca
@joffrecreekcabins
Accommodates 2–5 | Pets welcome

THE JOSHUA TREE FOLLY
(page 318)
Twentynine Palms, California
follycollection.com | @follycollection
Accommodates 6

JUST OUT OF NASHVILLE
(page 39)
Smithville, Tennessee
airbnb.com/rooms/23578827
@justoutofnashville
Accommodates 8

KNOWLTON AND CO. TREEHOUSE (page 80)
Durham, Ontario, Canada
lynneknowlton.com/treehouse-cabin
  -retreat | @knowltonandco
Accommodates 8

LA CABIN RIDE & SLEEP
(page 203)
Lac-Beauport, Ontario, Canada
lacabin.info | @lacabinrideandsleep
Accommodates 6

LAGÖM (page 180)
Lac-Beauport, Quebec, Canada
montagnelemaelstrom.com/en/lagom/
@montagne_lemaelstrom
Accommodates 4

LAKE O'HARA LODGE (page 246)
Yoho National Park, British Columbia,
  Canada
lakeohara.com/lodging/lake-shore
  -cabins
Accommodates 2–4

THE LAZY DUCK (page 69)
Inverness-shire, Scotland
lazyduck.co.uk | @thelazyduck
Accommodates 2–5

LITTLE OWL CABIN (page 86)
Packwood, Washington State
littleowlcabin.com | @littleowlcabin
Accommodates 5 | Pets welcome

LIVE OAK TREEHOUSE (page 107)
Fredericksburg, Texas
honeytreefbg.com | @honeytreefbg
Accommodates 2

LOOKING GLASS TREEHOUSE
(page 66)
Red River Gorge, Kentucky
rrgcabin.com | @canopycrew
Accommodates 6 | Pets welcome

MAISON TETONIA (page 215)
Tetonia, Idaho
airbnb.com/rooms/31085353
@maisontetonia
Accommodates 4

THE NOOQ (page 216)
Whitefish, Montana
thenooq.com | @thenooq
Accommodates 6

OLIVER LODGE A-FRAME
(page 257)
Meredith, New Hampshire
oliverlodge.com | @oliverlodgenh
Accommodates: 6

ORCA ISLAND CABINS (page 258)
Humpy Cove and Resurrection Bay,
   Seward, Alaska
orcaislandcabins.com
@orcaislandcabins
Accommodates 4

OREGON COAST MODERN
(page 262)
Manzanita, Oregon
oregoncoastmodern.com
@oregoncoastmodern
Accommodates 6

OUR JUNGLE HOUSE (page 131)
Surat Thani, Thailand
khaosokaccommodation.com
@ourjunglehouse
Accommodates 2–5

PANORAMA GLASS LODGE
(page 231)
Hella, Iceland
panoramaglasslodge.com
@panoramaglasslodge
Accommodates 2 | Pets welcome

PARC OMEGA (page 89)
Montebello, Quebec, Canada
parcomega.ca | @parcomega
Accommodates 4

THE PEAK HOUSE (page 194)
Mount Skuta, Kamnik-Savinja Alps,
   Slovenia
en.pzs.si
Accommodates 8 | Pets welcome

PHOENIX HOUSE (page 121)
Pahōa, Big Island, Hawaii
airbnb.com/rooms/plus/18551788
@artistree_treehouse
Accommodates: 2

PLATBOS FOREST CABINS
(page 51)
Gansbaai, Western Cape, South Africa
platbos.co.za | @platbosforest
Accommodates 2

THE POND HOUSE (page 286)
Phillipsport, New York
airbnb.com/rooms/40777064
@pond.place
Accommodates 6 | Pets welcome

PUMPHOUSE POINT (page 280)
Lake Saint Clair, Tasmania, Australia
pumphousepoint.com.au
@pumphousepoint
Accommodates 2 | Pets welcome

RED MOUNTAIN ALPINE LODGE
(page 162)
Ouray, Colorado
redmountainalpinelodge.com
@redmtnalpinelodge
Accommodates 22

RIVER CABAAN (page 290)
Tillamook, Oregon
airbnb.com/rooms/19863838
@rivercabaan
Accommodates 5

RIVIÈRE CABIN (page 285)
Mont-Tremblant, Quebec, Canada
@rivierecabin
Accommodates 10

SHELDON MOUNTAIN HOUSE
(page 236)
Ruth Glacier, Alaska
sheldonchalet.com | @sheldonchalet
Accommodates 6

SKYCABIN (page 46)
Skykomish, Washington State
airbnb.com/rooms/39119065
@skycabin.co
Accommodates 4

STONE CITY TREEHOUSE
(page 115)
Hardwick, Vermont
stonecitytreehouse.com
@stonecityvermont
Accommodates 2 | Pets welcome

SYÖTE IGLOOS (page 241)
Pudasjärvi, Finland
syoteigloos.fi | @syoteigloos
Accommodates 4

TAOS GOJI ECO LODGE
(page 323)
San Cristobal, New Mexico
airbnb.com/rooms/22992137
@taosgoji
Accommodates: 4 | Pets welcome

TINY CATSKILL CABIN (page 112)
Kerhonkson, New York
airbnb.com/rooms/plus/21911786
@tinycatskillcabin
Accommodates 6 | Pets welcome

TREEHOUSE A-FRAME (page 14)
Shasta County, California
treehouse.ourvie.com
@treehouseaframe
Accommodates 4

THE TREEHOUSE UTAH (page 198)
Park City, Utah
airbnb.com/rooms/3635074
@thetreehouseutah
Accommodates 2

TREELOFT (page 77)
Perryville, Missouri
airbnb.com/rooms/44119404
@basecampatcedarfork
Accommodates 2

TRIANGLE SIARGAO (page 134)
General Luna, Siargao Island,
   Philippines
airbnb.com/rooms/21541814
@thetriangle.siargao
Accommodates 2 | Pets welcome

TRUE NORTH CABIN (page 249)
Keweenaw Peninsula, Michigan
truenorthcabin.com
@true.north.cabin
Accommodates 4

TWIN PINES CHALET (page 72)
Big Bear, California
airbnb.com/rooms/41916633
@twinpineschalet
Accommodates 4

TYE RIVER CABIN CO. (page 62)
Skykomish, Washington State
tyerivercabinco.com | @tyehaus
Accommodates 4 | Pets welcome

WHISKEY CREEK CABIN
(page 101)
Idyllwild—Pine Cove, California
airbnb.com/rooms/33246578
@whiskeycreekcabin
Accommodates 4 | Pets welcome

WILLOW TREEHOUSE (page 310)
Willow, New York
airbnb.com/rooms/13761529
@treehousewillow
Accommodates 2

WOODHOUSE MUSKOKA
(page 25)
Coldwater, Ontario, Canada
cottagesincanada.com/26509
@thewoodhousemuskoka
Accommodates 8 | Pets welcome

WOODLAND CHASE TREEHOUSE
(page 52)
Felton, Northumberland, England
woodlandchaseglamping.co.uk
@woodlandchaseglamping
Accommodates 2

ZION ECO-CABIN (page 331)
Hurricane, Utah
airbnb.com/rooms/24873113
@zionecocabins
Accommodates: 2 | Pets welcome

Alpenglow Cabin, page 138

Woodhouse Muskoka,
page 25

ACKNOWLEDGMENTS

In 2015, I randomly started posting cabin pictures to an Instagram account. I had no particular goal, and certainly no idea what would happen next. I just knew that I loved cabins, and posting them seemed like the next logical step given all of the photos I was accruing. The "next" was discovering that there were thousands of other like-minded, cabin-obsessed folks out there. I even started to recognize the names of photographers as their pictures began to pop up and get shared with me. This book wouldn't exist without the followers of (nay, community!) and contributors to the @TheCabinChronicles page. Thank you, all.

I would like to thank my wife, Lizzie, who is a hardworking mother and nurse, for her support of my taking the time to construct this book during a very tough year. I would also like to thank my father, may he rest in peace, who always pushed me to do more and do it right the first time; my mother, whose energy and zeal for life is endlessly inspiring; and my siblings, for a lifetime of adventures.

A special thanks to the cabin owners and photographers who collaborated with me on this project, as well as to the book's phenomenal writer, Alexis Lipsitz. Your work brought these pages to life.

And to our editor, Bridget Monroe Itkin, who stayed on me to complete this project, providing encouragement on some hard days. You didn't really know what I was going through, and sometimes believed in this project more than I did.

Alexis and I would like to thank Artisan's publisher, Lia Ronnen, and a very fine team that includes Sibylle Kazeroid, Paula Brisco, Liana Faughnan, Elise Ramsbottom, Nina Simoneaux, Suet Chong, Annie O'Donnell, Nancy Murray, Hanh Le, Allison McGeehon, Theresa Collier, Amy Michelson, and Patrick Thedinga— as well as Michelle Wolfe and Kate Osba of Look See Photo.

And finally, I'd like to thank whisky.

—JJ Eggers

First of all, I want to express my respect and deep admiration for JJ Eggers. He started this thing from nothing, and his unerring eye and generous heart guided this project. His cabin wanderlust is absolutely infectious.

Second, I'd like to acknowledge our editor, Bridget Monroe Itkin, whose finesse as an editor is matched only by her unflappable good nature. She's a rock and a rock star. And I'd like to give a nod to my agent, Kitty Cowles, for her friendship and wise counsel.

Lastly, I want to give a shout-out to my pandemic mates, Royce and Maisie, who made life in our little Manhattan foxhole more than bearable. This is for you.

—Alexis Lipsitz

GENERAL INDEX

LOCATION INDEX

PHOTOGRAPHY CREDITS

Page 215 (top): Stephanie Miller
Page 215 (bottom): Nikki Lazaran
Pages 217–21: Alex Strohl
Page 222: Dhaval Patel
Page 227: Jack Ansley
Page 228: Iver Paulsberg
Page 229: Benedikt Huck
Pages 230 and 232–35: Courtesy Panorama
    Glass Lodge
Pages 240 and 242–43: Jarcce Oy
Pages 244 and 252: @mikestravelbook/
    Michael Hausmann
Page 246: Jackson De Matos
Pages 248, 250, and 291–93:
    Bennett Young
Page 251: Riutta Images
Pages 254–55: Studio Chevojon
Page 256: Matthew Zeng
Pages 263–65: Courtesy Oregon
    Coast Modern

Pages 267–69: Nicole Alex Photography
Page 270: Courtesy Emerald Lake Lodge
Pages 276 and 278–79: Nils Petter Dale
Pages 281: Stu Gibson
Pages 282–83: Adam Gibson
Pages 295: Becca Waterloo
Pages 296 and 298–300: Aimee Mazzenga
Page 297: Bob Coscarelli
Page 301: Sveta Damiani
Pages 307–9, 316, and 330: Ethan Abitz
Pages 311–15: Peter Crosby
Pages 332–33: Shutterstock
Pages 319–21: Sam Frost
Pages 322 and 324–25: Tina Larkin
Pages 327–29: Brian Smirke
Page 352: Torah Eggers
Back cover (top): Courtesy Lagöm

JJ EGGERS is the founder of the Instagram account @TheCabinChronicles, featuring images of the most amazing cabins around the world. Eggers is based out of Salt Lake City, Utah, where he and his family enjoy exploring the unique geography of the region.